"This brave book offers a psychologically attentive and practical theological anthropology that can serve as a guide for navigating the challenging, traumatic, and rewarding dimensions of border existence among family and friends; in ethnic, racial, and interfaith communities; and in global relations."

—Bradford Hinze
Fordham University

"Human beings are conscious selves, with constantly developing personal identities, intrinsically related to, acted upon, and affected by others in dynamic social, political, and religious spheres. Michele Saracino shows with exquisite sensitivity how these relationships are most tellingly revealed in human affectivity and emotions. Human existence entails ceaseless negotiation on all levels and requires 'reflective affectivity' to succeed. In this interdisciplinary work, which includes theology, ethics, politics, and psychology, Saracino penetrates to the core of the human in a highly original way and sheds brilliant light on our being in today's world. All will learn from this book."

—Roger Haight, SJ
Scholar in Residence
Union Theological Seminary

"Pastorally sensitive and psychologically astute, *Being about Borders* argues that genuinely transformative engagement with human difference must attend to the affective as well as the physical and cognitive dimensions of the self. Drawing on a range of examples from personal psychology, interreligious dialogue, and geopolitics, Saracino shows how attention to the borders of our individual and collective worlds is crucial if we are to do justice to the fullness of human experience in our encounters with others. Her passionate insistence on the need for patient, disciplined vigilance in attending to the emotional 'border traffic' between ourselves and those around us is accompanied by a consistently practical perspective that keeps her vision firmly anchored in the everyday. A thoughtful and serious proposal for deeply personal engagement in an increasingly fragmented and all too often impersonal world."

—Ian A. McFarland
Associate Professor of Systematic Theology
Emory University, Atlanta

Being about Borders

A Christian Anthropology of Difference

Michele Saracino

A Michael Glazier Book

LITURGICAL PRESS
Collegeville, Minnesota

www.litpress.org

A Michael Glazier Book published by Liturgical Press

Cover design by David Manahan, OSB.
Image from Liquid Library with Photos.com.

1	2	3	4	5	6	7	8	9

Library of Congress Cataloging-in-Publication Data

Saracino, Michele, 1971–
    Being about borders : a Christian anthropology of difference / Michele Saracino.
        p.   cm.
    "A Michael Glazier book."
    Includes bibliographical references (p.   ) and index.
    ISBN 978-0-8146-5710-2 (pbk.) — ISBN 978-0-8146-8005-6 (e-book)
    1. Theological anthropology—Christianity.   2. Other (Philosophy)
3. Christian sociology.   4. Cultural pluralism.   I. Title.

BT702.S27 2011
270.08—dc22

2010042291

For Ken, Roman, and Penelope,
who lovingly call me to be about borders everyday.

Contents

Acknowledgments

There are so many special people who have contributed to this book in one way or another. I would like to thank Manhattan College for supporting me throughout the years and for the sabbatical and summer grants that allowed for the completion of this project. My colleagues in the Religious Studies and English Departments have been indispensible with encouragement and friendship, inspiring me to think in new directions. Natalia Imperatori-Lee, Stephen Kaplan, Judith Plaskow, and Claudia Setzer were particularly helpful in providing sources, thinking through material with me, and reading sections of the text. My students throughout the years at Manhattan College have challenged me to grow, and I have them in mind much of the time when imagining what it takes to be about borders.

There are friends at other institutions I would like to acknowledge. Susan Abraham, M. Shawn Copeland, Cathy Cornell, Jeannine Hill Fletcher, Anthony Godzieba, Roger Haight, Christine Firer Hinze, Paul Lakeland, Elena Procario-Foley, and John Thiel have been instrumental in assisting me with this project in any number of ways, including reading through parts of the project, providing me with references, and generously supporting me throughout the years. The creativity and productivity of colleagues in the Workgroup in Constructive Theology have motivated me to push on when I became weary. I am particularly grateful for the years of friendship with Brad Hinze, who has read the entire manuscript in various forms, and supported me personally and professionally since my days in the doctoral program at Marquette University. Hans Christoffersen at Liturgical Press has been wonderful, warm, and encouraging from start to finish, and I am so appreciative of his time and efforts.

Closer to home, I offer a great sigh of relief and heartfelt thanks to my husband Ken Einhorn, who has read far too much theology for a psychologist and has introduced me to just enough psychology for a theologian. His care and concern for me, this project, and our life project together is incredible. My children Roman and Penelope were born during the time it has taken to complete this book, and their fingerprints are implicitly on its pages. I cherish the time I spend with them and hope I have not pushed them away from my computer too much! My longtime friends Elizabeth Bunn and Terri Maiorino have been there for me through all my personal and professional ups and downs, and I treasure their support and camaraderie. Finally, I want to thank my mother, Phyllis Saracino, who not only has labored through reading parts of this work but also was a constant source of support and care for my beautiful children, which allowed me to write this book in the first place. She is the inspiration for my reading of maternity as hybrid and unwittingly invited me into my first adventures in border life.

Parts of this book have appeared in earlier versions in books and articles. I gratefully acknowledge permission to use excerpts from the following:

"Hybridity and Trespass: With Jesus at the Borders of Identity," *Horizons* 33, no. 2 (Fall 2006): 221–38. Used with permission.

"Feeling through the Limits of Conversation," 103–11. Used with permission of The Crossroad Publishing Company. *Prophetic Witness: Catholic Women's Strategies for Reform*, edited by Colleen M. Griffith, Crossroad 2009.

"Moving Beyond the 'One True Story,'" in *Frontiers in Catholic Feminist Theology: Shoulder to Shoulder*, edited by Susan Abraham and Elena Procario-Foley (Minneapolis: Fortress Press, 2009), 9–24. Used with permission.

Introduction

We live in a culture in which we constantly hear that borders are disappearing. Whether the message is broadcast in the news, relayed through political campaigns, or even preached at local churches, the story is the same. Globalization has broken down boundaries between individuals, communities, and nations to the extent that those we used to consider alien and different from us are now part of our world.[1] Sometimes the same message is put more eloquently, that in the midst of human diversity we are all part of one unified world. Either way such rhetoric obscures the lived reality that borders are present everywhere—within interpersonal relationships, interreligious communities, and the international panorama. Is it feasible to argue that borders no longer exist between ethnic groups when some communities cannot stomach the odor of another's food or when one community raises their children in a way that is unconscionable to another? Is it really the case that borders are disappearing between religions when Jews and Catholics may be marrying each other and having children together but are still feeling the same tensions that interfaith couples experienced decades ago? Finally, how is it possible to fathom that borders are disappearing in the

---

[1] For an important theoretical reading of the dissolution of seemingly impermeable borders in the contemporary era, see Michael Hardt and Antonio Negri, *Empire* (Cambridge, MA: Harvard University Press, 2000). There they highlight the shift in the global political economy from being built on the idea of imperialism, which fosters clear boundaries, to empire, which "establishes no territorial center of power and does not rely on fixed boundaries or barriers" (xii). If one accepts their claims, the shift to empire makes realizing and interpreting difference even more involved than in an age of imperialism because there are no clear signifiers to denote alterity.

1

global landscape when some countries, including the United States of America, are more preoccupied than ever with closing doors to immigrants and refugees? Language about the global village cannot wish away the entrenched emotional responses to difference that we feel on a daily basis.

Surely it is desirable to imagine the world as getting smaller and practically borderless because then we do not have to feel so obligated to the others in our homes, communities, and nations. After all, a world without borders means a world without difference and all the complicated emotions that accompany living with others.[2] If, however, our feelings tell us otherwise, that there are others in our midst, then human beings have no choice but to acknowledge, respect, and manage borders. Christians in particular have an urgent call to be vigilant about borders, since they witness to a messiah who tirelessly seeks out the other at the margins and revels in border life. Jesus reaches out to the sick, the outcast, and the untouchables, and, in taking on the Christian story, we are called to do the same. There is one problem. While the gospels certainly provide an entrée into thinking about the complexity of dealing with others, they do not provide concrete strategies for navigating the unexpected and complicated feelings involved in our encounters with difference. Christians today need to find ways to engage these confusing and emotionally volatile border situations.

The disconnect between what one is supposed to do when faced with those who are different and what one in all probability feels when encountering others becomes strikingly clear for me when teaching undergraduates about Christian themes of hospitality and table fellowship. It is not unusual for me to emphasize Jesus as a messiah who expects his followers to invite all types of people to their social gatherings and into their communities. I often ask students to turn to the Gospel of Luke for a glimpse of Jesus' other-oriented message: "When you give a luncheon or a dinner, do not invite your friends or your brothers or your relatives or rich neighbors, in case they may invite you in return, and you would be repaid. But when you give a banquet, invite the poor, the crippled, the lame, and the blind. And you will be blessed, because they cannot repay you, for you will be repaid at the resurrection of the righteous" (Luke 14:12-14). After taking a few moments to explain the biblical pas-

---

[2] William T. Cavanaugh also cautions readers about this popular but misleading rhetoric about borders disappearing; see "Migrant, Tourist, Pilgrim, Monk: Mobility and Identity in a Global Age," *Theological Studies* 69, no. 2 (2008): 340–56.

sage, I then ask students to construct what such an alternative meal would look like in our day and age. Every semester at least one brave student volunteers and proceeds to the blackboard, beginning to map out a seating chart for this hypothetical get-together. Almost always, tables comprised of homeless people, those suffering from addictions, and persons faced with various mental and physical challenges emerge. Almost always, a few students blurt out, "What a depressing party!" Quickly it becomes apparent that speaking among one another at this event would be really challenging and perhaps even uncomfortable. In all likelihood, negative emotional reactions to those considered different would arise, including fear, anger, sadness, and anxiety.

Theological anthropology today more than ever needs to take into account the complicated emotional situations of being in relations of intense proximity with others, of being about borders. This urgency is not because emotions are more complicated or volatile than they used to be; on the contrary, falling prey to the assumption that within this new global reality borders are disappearing and hence difference is disappearing, one may begin to believe that their emotional reactions to difference are dissipating as well and hence not worthy of attention. This oversight can be catastrophic, and, if unchecked, long-standing negative visceral reactions to otherness could fester and incite violence. In order to avoid this trap, Christians need an added layer to their lenses for seeing what is at stake in their dealings with the other—one that reveals the nuances of the emotional impact of border life. As long as we ignore our feelings toward difference—the positive or the negative ones and even the ones somewhere in the middle—we cannot engage those who are different in life-giving ways. It is not enough to say that we are all different and as a result have nothing to talk about, or that we are all the same and thus have everything to celebrate. Instead, we must honor the reality that we are hybrid individuals and groups with a plurality of stories that overlap and intertwine with one another, leading to operatic moments that need to be embraced in order for genuine and life-giving relationships to develop.

In this book, I attempt to advance a theological anthropology of difference that above all else privileges the affectively charged dimensions of human existence, one that I call *being about borders*. Implicit in this anthropology is the argument that human existence cannot be interpreted in terms of knowledge or freedom alone; it must be read with vigilance about how human cognition and volition are shaped by affect. Clinical research, specifically that of trauma theory and treatment, can help us conceive of Christian notions of the human person that appreciate the affective component of being human. What is particularly unique about an affective understanding of theological anthropology is both that it confronts the challenges to difference posed by globalization and, moreover, that it hopes to undo at least some of the insidious dualism in Christianity and secular culture, which subordinates emotion to reason. Religious and cultural manifestations of dualism are damaging as they concretize gendered, racial, and any number of other bifurcated relationships, leading to inequitable power dynamics in both ecclesial and secular communities. Thus, in addition to complicating our commonsense rhetoric about borders and globalization, attending to the emotional impact of living with others at the borders can open up the conversation for thinking about models of human existence beyond the limiting binaries of self/other, male/female, black/white, Jew/Christian, victim/perpetrator, and so on.

Throughout the twentieth century and beyond, many theologians have focused on the interplay between emotion and corporeality in religious experience. In relation to theological anthropology, Bernard Lonergan highlights the importance of feeling in religious conversion and also emphasizes the role of affect in moving toward and participating in what he calls the "human good."[3] Pushing Lonergan's theology, Robert Doran explains a next level of "psychic conversion" that "enables" one to "narrate" the feelings and "drama" of his or her life in order to achieve authenticity.[4] Furthermore, Bradford Hinze's work on dialogical ecclesiology calls for attention to the complicated emotional issues behind our "laments" in our encounters with and among others.[5] Contemporary European theologians practicing "communicative theology" incorporate psychoanalytic techniques into their theological processes thereby highlighting the importance of affect in understanding what it means to be Christian.[6] And, of course, black, feminist, womanist, Latino/a, and queer theologians for decades now have shown the need for honesty

[3] Bernard J. F. Lonergan, *Method in Theology* (Toronto: University of Toronto Press, 1990), esp. pp. 30–33.

[4] Robert M. Doran, *Subject and Psyche*, 2nd ed. (Milwaukee: Marquette University Press, 1994), 243.

[5] Bradford E. Hinze, *Practices of Dialogue in the Roman Catholic Church: Aims and Obstacles, Lessons and Laments* (New York: Continuum, 2006).

[6] See Matthias Scharer and Bernd Jochen Hilberath, *The Practice of Communicative Theology: Introduction to a New Theological Culture* (New York: Crossroad Publishing Co., 2008).

about the matrix of connections among theology, embodied experience, and feelings of fear and anger, especially in regard to situations of oppression.[7] One of the great contributions of these liberationist theologies is the simple claim that all theology is contextual, that is, all are based in individual and communal needs, feelings, memories, and stories.[8] My work is deeply indebted to and driven by these theological voices and strives to continue in line with them by constructing a theological anthropology of difference based in our affective responses to one another.

In thinking through the emotional impact of living with others, the notion of "borders" emerges as a protean theme.[9] For some, "borders" has become a defining characteristic of identity. According to Roberto Goizueta, "For Latinos and Latinas, the border is not only *where* we are located, or *where* we come from; the border is *who* we are, people whose very identity and reality is 'in between.' "[10] Here, the "border" is not "merely a geographic category but is, more profoundly, an epistemological and anthropological category."[11] I agree that borders can serve as a lens for understanding human life and relationship, and I imagine borders not in terms of a specific identity for any one specific group but rather more in regard to how they mark an encounter with difference, which creates an emotional response. Some of the borders that will be explored here include those between parents and children, ethnic and religious groups, and nations and political entities. Once one becomes comfortable with being vigilant about the emotional impact of borders in each of these contexts, other border situations will undoubtedly come to mind. Whatever the border, I assert that each one of us has a responsibility to "be about borders," or in other words, each one of us is chosen

[7] For example, see M. Shawn Copeland, *Enfleshing Freedom: Body, Race, and Being* (Minneapolis: Fortress Press, 2010), for a stunning analysis of the way that power unfolds in the particular embodied stories and histories of black women, and the implications of those stories for our being human today.

[8] For an important synthesis of many of these liberation theologies and their impact on our everyday experience, see Elizabeth A. Johnson, *Quest for the Living God: Mapping Frontiers in the Theology of God* (New York: Continuum, 2007).

[9] Throughout this book I use the terms "border" and "boundary" interchangeably.

[10] Roberto S. Goizueta, "'There You Will See Him': Christianity Beyond the Frontier Myth," in *The Church as Counterculture*, ed. Michael L. Budde and Robert W. Brimlow (Albany: SUNY Press, 2000), 176.

[11] Ibid., 177.

to be attentive to the emotional impact of borders so that life-affirming relationships of difference can flourish.

My use of the term "being" in describing this anthropology—this being about borders—may be unsettling for some, as there is an undeniable rationalist connotation associated with the term "being." Throughout history, being has been equated with thinking and with the life of the mind, leading to a dualism between mind and body that I so fiercely reject. In an attempt to counter this dualistic trap, I entertained the idea of using the phrase "feeling about borders." Nevertheless, that phrase has the potential to undermine my thesis altogether, which is that being human is an activity that involves three corporeal dimensions—thinking, doing, and feeling—the last of which has been and continues to be occluded for any number of the aforementioned reasons. I want to illuminate the way feeling frames our thinking and acting; however, I do not want to erase the importance of human thought and action.

Others may resist my use of the word "being" because they think I have a particular concept of the human being in mind or even that I am striving to develop an overarching theory about human existence. On all accounts I avoid any grand theorizing of being. Much of my work is permeated implicitly if not explicitly by the thought of Emmanuel Levinas, a Jewish thinker who has critiqued the paralyzing and objectifying effects of ontology, specifically that of Martin Heidegger's work.[12] My intentions here thus are not to communicate one fixed system of being, but to underscore the notion that being human in a way that honors the gospels, the person and work of Christ, and God's relationship with creation is a complicated arduous spiritual *process*—one that demands an inestimable amount of work, specifically an incessant vigilance about the emotional overflow that accompanies living with others.

Overview of the Chapters

I have divided this book into six chapters, the first of which lays the groundwork for understanding the reasons why many of us are troubled by borders in the midst of hybrid existence. The main problem is not that borders are disappearing but that they are becoming more porous and less definable. The more we interact with others from previously

---

[12] For Emmanuel Levinas's most comprehensive critique of ontology see, *Otherwise than Being or Beyond Essence*, trans. Alphonso Lingis (Pittsburgh: Duquesne University Press, 1998).

disparate worlds, the more the boundaries of our identities overlap and intertwine with one another. Our stories leak onto and sometimes become enmeshed with that of another, resulting in what I have already referred to as hybrid existence. Porous borders lead to hybridity. The trouble with borders is that while the term "porous" in and of itself is innocuous, more often than not borders' porous qualities cause negative feelings. And in those times, when we find ourselves responding out of control emotionally, we no longer are okay with borders and their porosity. In fact, we do everything and anything to fix those leaky borders and put an end to the emotional onslaught that their permeability brings.

If we are going to be committed to inviting others to our table, nevertheless, we need to grapple with this unexpected and unregulated affect endemic to hybrid existence. This is far from easy, as there are at least three typical adverse emotional reactions to such porous borders, any of which, if unchecked, could have disastrous effects. The first and most obvious emotional response to porous borders is when people fear the other so intensely that they do anything and everything to avoid them. Another response to borders is when people feel entitled to them to the extent that they cannot acknowledge the self, story, or place of the other at the border. Arguably, the most insidious reaction to borders appears when individuals or communities become anesthetized to feelings at borders because of a past trauma. Their numbness to affect prevents them from detecting and opening to others in charity. Clearly, none of these approaches are appropriate or helpful since none embody the affective openness needed to be about borders in a globalized world.

In chapter 2, I outline various Christian theological resources, or what I call "talking points," that can help believers negotiate the affective responses to border life. Both in theological claims about creation and about the person and work of Jesus Christ, one can find fresh avenues for navigating hybrid existence. Through fleshing out these theological claims, practical strategies for dealing with otherness emerge, including becoming ready and comfortable with conflict, showing one's vulnerability, and, most important, creating a place in one's spiritual journey for mourning. This last strategy, mourning, is an indispensable act in the process of being human—not the final one, but one nonetheless that precipitates the conversion necessary for being vigilant about otherness in the midst of a world of "moving and mixing."[13] If people acknowledge

---

[13] Hubert J. M. Hermans and Harry J.G. Kempen, "Moving Cultures: The Perilous Problems of Cultural Dichotomies in a Globalizing Society," *American Psychologist* 53, no. 10 (1998): 1117.

their identity as hybrid, they have to admit to having plural stories as well as to the reality that some of their stories overlap and perhaps conflict with others. They have to surrender and mourn the "one true story" they often use as a security blanket when dealing with others. Beyond mourning, then, Christians can hope for renewed relationship and reconciliation with the other, although that is not often immediate or readily foreseeable.

In the third chapter, I apply the practical strategies of conflict, exposure, and mourning to several aspects of our interpersonal border encounters. First, I reflect on the ways in which we understand ourselves in relation to another through stories about our bodies. Considering bodily borders, maternity emerges as a metaphor for imagining what it takes to live at the emotionally volatile borders among self, other, and all the hybridized spaces in-between. Accordingly, I posit pregnancy as a moment in which it becomes strikingly clear that accepting the responsibility of hybrid existence demands more than celebrating the fact that human beings are composed of many stories; it also involves deciphering which of those stories will engender life-flourishing relationships with others at the border and relinquishing those that do not. Continuing with borders within family, I explore more generally the emotional tenor of border relationships between parents and their children, focusing on the ways in which parents choose to relate to their children, as an authority or as a friend. Finally, our interpersonal encounters with others in relation to our ethnic identities are discussed.

In the fourth chapter, I continue to prioritize the emotional implications of border life and the need for conflict, exposure, and mourning, this time within the communal, interreligious context of Jewish-Catholic relations. Ecclesial decrees and arguments about the need to foster the familial relationship between Jews and Christians have been at the forefront of Catholic consciences since the Second Vatican Council. Nonetheless, few have been attentive to the affectively charged dimensions of what some might consider a sibling rivalry. In returning to fundamental church documents and interrogating the recent canonization of Edith Stein, I argue that the most charitable way for Catholics to live at the borders with their Jewish sisters and brothers may be to heed the emotional needs of the Jewish community rather than push any doctrinal affirmations about what is good, true, and salvific. Stein's life stories, specifically those related to her being a Catholic convert from Judaism who became a Carmelite nun and was murdered at Auschwitz, raise all sorts of questions about how to acknowledge, respect, and manage borders between religious communities that are becoming increasingly porous. The issues raised in this chapter can facilitate thinking about borders in other interreligious contexts, encompassing the much debated and contested question of how to maintain Catholic identity on the institutional level. While I cannot and do not attend to every border encounter, it is my hope that readers employ these test cases as models for imagining how to be about borders within their own contexts.

The family metaphor that surfaces in my discussion of interpersonal and interreligious borders carries over to chapter 5 where I explore two highly politicized international border disputes. I begin with an analysis of Israeli-Palestinian border negotiations, demonstrating that much of the emotional drama surrounding their border life is colored by projections about their characters and their plural stories. In fact, many of our actions in the face of encountering someone different are shaped by stories we have either heard or told about them, including how they are a threat to us or have hurt us in some life-altering way. A substantial section of this chapter is focused on the importance of relinquishing all claims to having the right story at the border and all beliefs affirming that one is permanently victimized by the other. The rhetoric of injury is quite prevalent in international relations as various parties in dispute often cling to the role of victim, employing it to rationalize and legitimize any questionable or unethical behavior on one's part. This rhetoric needs to be challenged, surrendered, and even mourned for more life-giving dynamics between different groups to emerge, those that embrace overlapping stories, memories, and feelings, honoring hybrid existence. It is important to note that in this chapter I do not stay within the sphere of Israeli-Palestinian relations; rather, I employ those border disputes to set the stage for imagining what being about borders might mean for Christians living in the United States in a post-9/11 era, where so much of the public conversation about living with others is framed by the discourse of fearing terrorists and terrorism.

Through exploring the affective impact of borders in a handful of test cases within our interpersonal, interreligious, and international affairs, it becomes apparent that in order to follow the gospel mandate to live with others, one has no other option but to negotiate complicated emotional situations. In the final chapter, then, I propose that trauma treatment can help Christians navigate the affective dissonance of border life. In the latest clinical approaches to trauma, various body-based techniques that target the emotional and physiological aspects of suffering and injury are used in place of traditional talking cures. These somatic strategies have the potential to be incorporated successfully into a theological anthropology that respects the complexity of difference, one that opens emotionally to the other at the borders through conflict, exposure, and mourning. While I in no way am proposing that the church should be replaced by the clinic, I am asserting that the field of trauma studies has much to offer Christians invested in engaging difference and the ambivalent feelings otherness brings. Put simply, in a world with border trouble, living like Jesus requires more than thinking and doing; it also involves developing oneself emotionally.

A Word about Method

I write as a Catholic theologian with an interest and investment in other disciplines, including psychology, literary studies, and contemporary continental and postcolonial theories. These other fields provide alternative stories for illustrating what is at stake in theological anthropology today. Clinicians and theorists are my dialogue partners, those voices in my head, or, more fitting, those others at my table, to whom I pay close attention as I attempt to advance a theological anthropology for a global context. At times it may seem as if I move in and out of these other disciplines and discourses with a counterfeit license. After all, what gives me the right to use trauma treatment techniques in a book on theology? Or from an alternative angle, one is justified in asking, at what point is this a book on theology anymore? These are the potential pitfalls of broaching disciplinary boundaries, which makes some work difficult to categorize and label. The ways in which I cross discursive borders at some points might make someone feel uncomfortable. At times, I wonder myself about the implications of such trespass. Does one discipline become watered down or is one made subservient to the other? In all honesty, I cannot offer any simple answers here. This issue mirrors the thesis of my book, that we are always faced with otherness at borders, and we have a responsibility to admit, acknowledge, and manage them— even the ones among academic disciplines. I hope readers trust and engage in my conversational style, and talk back if and when it does not work. For me, that is what being about borders invokes.

Related to the topic of method is my relentless questioning of the emotional impact of every border engagement. I am grateful in advance for those who bear with me, as at times I narrate and process my own personal stories in an effort to flesh out very concretely what is at stake in being about borders. In utilizing such a subjective style, there is always a danger of revealing too much. When does it become superfluous or, even worse, when is it self-indulgent? Some may find themselves asking this same sort of question in the classroom or perhaps in an analogous situation. I can recall teaching a seminar on the topic of religion and the body in which each of the students in their own way risked their sense of self, story, and place at the table to meet that of another and at times to recognize themselves in that of another. The seminar discussion was highly subjective, and while there were required scholarly readings and other academic assignments, student participation was deeply personal and narrative based. At one point or another, each of the participants wondered about the role of personal story in the classroom. Yet when the storyteller connected with the material, one could feel the import of experience for the individual and for the community. This was by far one of the richest experiences I have ever had in the classroom, and anyone who has had this experience either as a teacher or as a student knows the gift of it. It is my hope that others will feel freed up to do similar types of storytelling in their theological encounters with others and otherness, beginning their own emotionally risk-filled journey of being about borders.

Chapter 1

The Trouble with Borders

It is comforting to idealize borders as secure and well-marked spaces that separate people, places, and things and, in turn, make our lives easier to navigate. The trouble with borders is that more often than not they are porous and indefinable, allowing for moving and mixing among them, even leading to confusion and triggering emotional distress. Consider the boundaries among the world's religions. Although creeds differentiate one religion from another, in our pluralist world there is a tendency for their borders to give way. As a result, one religious tradition might begin to converge with that of another, generating an ambiguous situation that could incite negative and divisive emotions, including anxiety, fear, anger, resentment, and rage. The emotionally unstable predicament due to leaky borders could also cause one to question the very foundation of their identity. How can one say anything definitive about what it means to be a Christian or what it means to be a Jew when the border between them is not secure? Identity confusion can manifest in any number of contexts even in relation to the way ethnic groups are categorized. What really makes one person Italian American and another African American? The more one probes the essence of borders, the more it becomes apparent that there is nothing at all certain about them; they are those places that are known only by what we feel in their proximity. Yet, it is the emotional impact of them—the very thing that signifies borders—that continues to be overlooked.

It is not that we avoid speaking about how borders are changing; on the contrary, popular rhetoric of our day speaks freely about globalization and our new hybrid reality. Much of our talk about pluralism nevertheless obscures the need for a sustained conversation about one's feelings in relation to this new reality. Just because we are encountering difference at an exponential rate these days does not mean we are not having any negative emotional reactions to it. To be sure, many of us today are more comfortable with difference than in the past, but there are moments for some of us in which we feel emotionally undone by the presence of another. Our new global reality, however, makes admitting this experience taboo—you just don't talk about those ugly and shameful feelings. When the prevailing assumption is that boundaries are disappearing, and as a result that we are all connected with one another, it becomes difficult to argue that we still feel difference.

If and when we do decide to take a risk and admit our negative emotional responses to the other, we chance being categorized as "behind the times" or, even worse, being thought of as prejudiced. It is precisely because of these assumptions regarding our new global reality that Christians need to take up a posture of being human that is vigilant about one's feelings in the face of another, so that they do not fester and escalate into situations of violence. The conflation of globalization with openness to others obscures the practical reality of living with those who are different in the midst of hybrid existence. If we are committed to being about borders, meaning engaging others with empathy and care, then in our age of hybridity we have no choice but to be attentive to borders, as porous as they may be, including the operatic emotions that permeate them. We have a responsibility to acknowledge what Gloria Anzaldúa notes as the "intimate terrorism" of borders and welcome it into our lives.[1]

Borders as Breeding Grounds for Hybridity

If borders are porous, then there is always a situation of moving and mixing among them, leading to an existence permeated by what some call "hybridity." Pinning down one clear definition of "hybridity" is tenuous at best as it has been employed in many different ways. I use the term "hybrid" to mean that our identities are comprised of many stories, including those related to our gender, ethnicity, class, race, sexual orientation, ability, and religion. We have been socialized into these

---

[1] Gloria Anzaldúa, *Borderlands/La Frontera: The New Mestiza* (San Francisco: Aunt Lute Books, 1987), 20.

stories from a young age and may or may not be aware totally of their impact on our being in relation to others.

The term "hybrid," however, has a long history. Few could forget Gregor Mendel's foundational genetic research on hybrid crossings in plant life.[2] More recently in the academic field of the humanities, post-colonialist theorists have invoked the notion of hybridity to signify identities that cannot be reduced to any one static homogenous concept, which coincides with my sense of hybrid in terms of having many stories.[3] Even world leaders strive to consider a hybrid sense of humanity. When the former senator from Illinois and now the forty-fourth president of the United States of America, Barack Obama, was under fire for being part of Reverend Jeremiah Wright's church, a pastor associated with what some have considered to be hate speech against white Americans, Obama, the son of a "black man" and a "white woman," responded by retelling his own hybrid story: "I can no more disown him [Rev. Wright] than I can disown the black community. I can no more disown him than I can disown my white grandmother, a woman who helped raise me, a woman who sacrificed again and again for me, a woman who loves me as much as she loves anything in this world, but a woman who once confessed her fear of black men who passed her by on the street, and who on more than one occasion has uttered racial or ethnic stereotypes that made me cringe. These people are a part of me."[4] Here, I echo strands of each of these perspectives, ultimately arguing that being hybrid means being composed of many stories, some of which overlap with others and some of which stand in sharp contrast with others. In order to be vigilant about borders, I hope to show that all human beings, and especially Christians, are obligated to reveal the enmeshed nature of human existence by exploring their feelings in order for more life-flourishing relationships to endure.

[2] Gregor Mendel, *Experiments in Plant-Hybridisation* (Cambridge, MA: Harvard University Press, 1938; orig. 1866).

[3] For his work on the importance of hybrid or the in-between spaces of identity in literature, semiotics, and culture, see Homi K. Bhabha, *The Location of Culture* (London: Routledge, 1994). For more analysis of hybridity, see Robert J. C. Young, *Colonial Desire: Hybridity in Theory, Culture and Race* (London: Routledge, 1995); and Samira Kawash, *Dislocating the Color Line: Identity, Hybridity, and Singularity in African-American Narrative* (Stanford: Stanford University Press, 1997).

[4] "Sen. Barack Obama Addresses Race at the Constitution Center in Philadelphia," *Washington Post*, March 18, 2008, http://www.washingtonpost.com/wp-dyn/content /article/2008/03/18/AR2008031801081.html (accessed March 21, 2008).

There is a danger in asserting that all individuals and groups must claim their hybridity. At first glance, it might read as if I am ignorant to the reality that everyone experiences hybridity uniquely. To be sure, for some, embracing their identity as hybrid is not a choice; rather, it is something they are forced to do and they are stigmatized because of it. Reading Gloria Anzaldúa's work on the painful experience of having grown up on the Texas-Mexico border and of being Chicana, it becomes apparent that hybridity cannot be conceptualized romantically, especially when many peoples and cultures are fragmented and broken by conquest and exile.[5] These hybrids are dehumanized and demonized by more powerful groups because they do not have "one pure story" or one idealized identity in their background. Other groups are robbed of the right to call themselves hybrid even if they wanted to claim the name. African Americans in many ways have been essentialized to such an extreme by white supremacist ideology that there is no room for them to be conceptualized as anything else than other, and, as such, being considered hybrid—that is, sharing stories with other less stigmatized groups—is out of their reach.[6] With particular attention to these experiences as well as of others, I argue against interpreting hybridity in any commonsense manner and instead propose that none of us are free from the responsibility of acknowledging our hybridity as well as that of others. Acknowledging our many-storied identities creates the possibility for us to meet and reach out to others with empathy and care.

In *The Practice of Everyday Life,* Michel de Certeau explains how story arranges one's sense of reality: "In modern Athens, the vehicles of mass transportation are called *metaphorai.* To go to work or come home, one takes a 'metaphor'—a bus or a train. Stories could also take this noble name: every day, they traverse and organize places; they select and link them together; they make sentences and itineraries out of them. They are spatial trajectories."[7] In the discourse of de Certeau, integral to being about borders is taking stock of the many stories that inform our lives, those that shape who we are, what we want out of life, and how we are

---

[5] See Anzaldúa, *Borderlands/La Frontera*; see also, Roberto S. Goizueta, *Caminemos con Jesús: Toward a Hispanic/Latino Theology of Accompaniment* (Maryknoll, NY: Orbis Books, 1995).

[6] See Victor Anderson, *Beyond Ontological Blackness: An Essay on African American Religious and Cultural Criticism* (New York: Continuum, 1995).

[7] Michel de Certeau, *The Practice of Everyday Life,* trans. Steven Rendall (Berkeley: University of California Press, 1984), 115.

connected to others. Quickly it becomes apparent that when interpreting human existence through narrative, the stories that inform our individual and group identities are always plural. Some of us are students, sons, and African Americans. Others of us are teachers, mothers, and Christians. We find ourselves playing a variety of roles and reciting a diversity of scripts all at the same time. As Jeannine Hill Fletcher argues, not defined exclusively by any one narrative, "we are all hybrids"—collections of various stories related to our life experiences, family origins, gender, class, religion, and so on.[8] The mere realization of this fact obligates us to surrender the one true story that brings us comfort, to acknowledge that our many-storied selves are connected to those of others at borders, and to face the affective floodgate that such a realization unhinges.

In employing the term "hybrid" in working toward a model of a Christian anthropology of difference, my aim is not to be faddish but rather to highlight the ethical implications of being human in a world with porous borders. Because we have many stories, we have a moral obligation to acknowledge that so do others. Moreover, acknowledging and embracing hybrid existence either on the individual or communal level entails heeding the other's story, memories, and feelings. It means revealing how your stories overlap even if you wished that they did not. It means being open to the conflictual, emotional reactions related to that revelation. Through converting to, or what I like to call "incarnating," hybridity, Christians are compelled to grapple with the many stories of themselves and that of another, as well as to the ambiguity of all the spaces in-between. These liminal places, as Homi Bhabha explains, "initiate new signs of identity, and innovative sites of collaboration, and contestation, in the act of defining the idea of society itself."[9]

Emotional Responses to Borders

Grappling with the emotional onslaught of borders within our hybrid existence is not without problems. Even with the best of intentions, Christians, like any other group, exhibit all sorts of adverse feelings and reactions when faced with others. Sometimes we fear difference so

[8] For a riveting analysis of hybridity in relation to encountering those from other faith traditions, see Jeannine Hill Fletcher, *Monopoly on Salvation? A Feminist Approach to Religious Pluralism* (New York: Continuum, 2005), 82–101.

[9] Bhabha, *The Location of Culture*, 1–2.

strongly that it prevents us from approaching the border altogether. Our apprehension about who or what is at the border could even result in our policing the boundary, so much so that there is no chance for genuine relationships with others to develop. Currently, the United States is experiencing this policing rather concretely, as raging debates about immigration legislation are forcing the government and citizens to choose sides for or against more intense border control. When someone does manage to cross the national border, they risk becoming a victim of hate crimes, which some might say is a less systematic yet far more violent form of policing boundaries.

Unfortunately, fear and policing are not the only issues at borders. At other times, our inability to detect others at the border leads to more border trouble. As already mentioned, the development of multinational corporations, transcontinental travel, and communication technology— the catalysts of globalization—have eroded the space between one another, making borders in many ways invisible. Yet, the force of my argument rests on the premise that while borders among individuals, communities, and even nations today might be difficult to pinpoint exactly, they do indeed exist. We know them because we feel them. When we refuse to admit they exist we run the risk of not acknowledging the presence of others and of privileging our feelings and needs over theirs in an entitled way. While fear and entitlement are certainly problematic, not feeling at all could quite possibly present as the most egregious approach to borders. This occurs when individual and cultural forms of narcissism cause one to become numb to the complexity of border life.

Feeling Scared at Borders

Due to their porosity, approaching a boundary of any sort raises many disturbing questions. Who is on the other side of the dividing line? Will they hurt me? What will trespass cost me, money or perhaps my life? All of these fears and apprehensions illuminate how borders signify a limit to one's comfort zone, places that we avoid or incessantly patrol in order to elude the emotional messiness of someone or something that is different. It would be wrong to over generalize here since some people are quite comfortable with difference and even thrive on it. For them borders are not troublesome at all and should not be cast in a negative light, particularly as they signify openings for creative and fecund relations. While the negative side of borders encompasses all our anxieties about the repercussions of encountering others, the positive side of borders is the way in which difference is maintained and relationships emerge in their midst, and that at times moving and mixing among them creates new identities and relationships. Even with their possibilities, few of us are content with the unknown factors that borders bring or with the limits they impose on our being. Instead of dealing openly with the emotional turmoil that borders stir, we run away from them or police them to the point of violence.

On too many occasions to count, avoiding and regulating boundaries has ended in tragedy. It is difficult to forget the death of college student Matthew Shepard who tried to live the way so many of us do, with complicated and multilayered stories. Arguably, his captors were more than merely uncomfortable with the way he crossed borders, or rather contested the border of heterosexuality, as his trespass was met with murder. One might say they dreaded the proximity of the other, never mind the potential for a hybridized existence with such a person, the fact that somehow all of their stories and thus their identities could be interconnected. Their fear led them to police boundaries of normative sexuality to the point of another's death.

There are other tragic stories like Shepard's. Less publicized was the murder of Gwen Araujo who in 2002 was found bludgeoned to death in Newark, California.[10] What was this seventeen year old's trespass? Gwen was in all probability so uncomfortable with the skin she was born and socialized into that she contested and renegotiated her bodily borders. Born Eddie Araujo Jr., Gwen eventually began to assume the identity of a woman. Not everyone was at ease with her decision; in fact, this teen's mere presence drove her peers to kill her. From the commentary surrounding her death, it appears that her murderers could not tolerate the risk of being with Gwen in the mix of the emotional messiness of border life. Vigilance was too costly for them, since it more than likely involved delving into their own hybridized stories about their gender identity. So instead they killed her, policing borders in violence.

These acts of violence are sometimes referred to as hate crimes. What I am suggesting here is that there is another way to conceptualize these brutal acts, namely, as border crimes—the injustices that occur when encountering difference. Even though it is common to think of borders as secure and well-defined markers, separating uncontested spaces,

---

[10] See Bob Moser, "The Murder of a Boy Named GWEN," *Rolling Stone* no. 968 (February 24, 2005): 60–65, *Academic Search Premier*, EBSCO*host* (accessed August 24, 2010).

many of us would agree that borders are more permeable than this. As a result, border crossings are always precarious. Christians know this as Jesus also transgressed the limits of place—a protest that was met with a similar fate to that of Shepard and Araujo. By escaping being constricted by any one category or story and reaching out to those deemed other in society, Jesus angered people to the point of his own demise.

Avoiding the other and policing borders to the point of violence is everywhere. Whether one is afraid to enroll their children into a certain school district or one thinks the United States should patrol its borders more rigorously, the emphasis is placed on monitoring one's personal and communal boundaries at the expense of the well-being of another. The compulsion to police boundaries is driven by the emotional confusion caused by their porosity. Not having a clear and definitive sense of the differences between one another creates a situation rife with ambiguity, one that has the potential to cause people to develop negative feelings and experience discomfort, forcing them to question everything about themselves, the other, and all the hybridized spaces in-between.

Feeling Entitled at Borders

While today it is common to feel scared at borders, it is just as prevalent to feel entitled to more than one needs or deserves at them. Feeling entitled can happen to anyone; moreover, some claim that consumerist culture fosters a particularly insidious form of the feeling. Robert J. Samuelson explains: "We [those living in the United States] feel entitled. Among other things, we expect secure jobs, rising living standards, enlightened corporations, generous government, high-quality health care, racial harmony, a clean environment, safe cities, satisfying work, and personal fulfillment. On the world stage, we think the United States should be the dominant political and economic power. Our political ideas ought to inspire societies everywhere; our industries should be the most efficient and innovative. Entitlement captures the full sweep of our feelings about America and its role in the world."[11] Entitlement evades inquiry into what is fair and just, holding onto instead a sense that something is expected and deserved. Moreover, it is conceivable that in consumerist capitalist culture, we come to identify ourselves most basically through our accumulation of land, objects, and even people.

---

[11] Robert J. Samuelson, *The Good Life and Its Discontents: The American Dream in the Age of Entitlement 1945–1995* (New York: Times Books/Random House, 1995), 4–5.

Part of the paradox of the prevailing attitude of entitlement is that one's expectation is more often than not unfulfilled. Very few people work in secure jobs, live in clean and safe cities, or experience racial harmony, leaving them disillusioned with life. In theory, pain and loss wield the potential to effect deeper reflection into one's feelings, hopes, and goals. Such self-interrogation seldom occurs, however, and instead of rethinking the attitude or the "American Fantasy" of entitlement, some argue that we begin to blame others for our unhappiness.[12] Holding another accountable for one's personal suffering has its limits in that it only temporarily satisfies the desire for control over one's life in this world of uncertainty: "Entitlement is a mirage. Its essence is the quest for control."[13] As entitlement points to an attitude that assumes one deserves this or that at all costs, it obscures the connection between working for something and earning it, thereby subverting the possibility of responsibility. The emphasis on the rights of the one entitled blinds him or her to the wants or, worse even, to the needs of others. Feelings of entitlement destroy one's capacity to be open to others emotionally or otherwise isolates them and forces them to believe in the commonsense logic that charity begins at home. Christians are called to maneuver the gray line of borders courageously in a posture of charity for the other.

CHARITY VERSUS ENTITLEMENT

Implicit in my work is a contrast between acting charitably at the borders and acting entitled. The choice is for all human beings to make, and for Christians it becomes a loaded question as they are called to live a life of love for others. It is noteworthy that what I mean by charity here is more than tolerance and more than giving what one is comfortable not having. It is those things and ultimately more—an affective openness to others—a willingness to participate in the risk-filled emotional give-and-take that defines the richest and the most complicated of our relationships. In framing charity as an openness to affect, one implicitly asserts that Jesus' message cannot be limited to thinking or acting for others but must also encompass feeling for others without assuming one can account for all the other's feelings. From a psychological perspective, this reading of charity might be thought of as empathy.

[12] Ibid., 16.
[13] Ibid., 49.

Much has been written from a Christian perspective on the connection between emotion and charity. Edward Vacek's work, *Love, Human and Divine: The Heart of Christian Ethics*, highlights the irreplaceable role of emotion in Christian life: "The history of Christianity is often told in terms of *orthodoxy*, the truth of doctrines believed; and Christians are frequently evaluated in terms of their *orthopraxy*, the good that they do. But the inner history of Christianity is what we might call its *orthokardia*, the ordered affections that unite us with God, ourselves, other people, and the world. These affections give rise to both doctrine and practice. Ultimately, our perfection as a person is measured strictly according to the degree of development of our loves."[14] While Vacek's work rigorously explores the complexity of the "activity" of emotion and how it binds us with self and others, in my work, I argue something more basic, namely, that being open to emotion at all, to the feelings of oneself and that of another, is in and of itself a gesture of charity. Such a gesture is not possible without vigilance about how one feels about another, about where those feelings originate, about whether they are life-giving, and if not, about how we can convert those negative feelings into expressions of charity. When we refuse to acknowledge emotion, we tread on closing ourselves to the other at the border in a posture of entitlement.

Not Feeling at Borders

So far I have discussed troublesome feelings that could potentially emerge when one approaches a border of any kind, focusing on feelings of fear and feelings of entitlement. These feelings often offend and hurt the others at the border, and thus need to be processed. Arguably there is an even worse impediment to imagining a constructive way to be about borders: not feeling at all. This numbness is a symptom of a larger clinical and cultural phenomenon referred to as narcissism. More than any other challenge to border life, narcissism needs to be treated in order for a model of human existence based on the affective give-and-take of our everyday hybridized relations to unfold.

In Ovid's *Metamorphoses*, Narcissus is the irresistible playboy who ends up paying an exorbitant price for his careless romantic escapades.[15]

---

[14] Edward Collins Vacek, *Love, Human and Divine: The Heart of Christian Ethics* (Washington, DC: Georgetown University Press, 1994), 5.

[15] Ovid, *Metamorphoses*, trans. Rolfe Humphries (Bloomington: Indiana University Press, 1983).

After he crosses the wrong person, Narcissus is cursed to find unrequited love with the next person he meets. Seeing his reflection in a pool of water, he becomes love-struck with himself and consequently wastes the remainder of his life imprisoned by his image. What is intriguing about this story is not that Narcissus is vain, what is sometimes implied by the term "narcissism," but rather his confusion of his reflection in the water with himself, in other words, his inability to grasp where he ends and the world begins. He is unable to be vigilant about difference in the midst of hybridity, in the midst of moving and mixing. In light of this myth, clinicians diagnose people who cannot recognize interpersonal boundaries with narcissism. Patients with narcissism are not cursed by the gods; perhaps, rather, their narcissism is due to childhood trauma, including that of neglect and abuse. Because memories associated with past interpersonal relationships become too painful to deal with, patients avoid intimate relations of many sorts, disassociating from their feelings as well as from the feelings of any others. Without being attentive to and embracing emotions, they lose sight of the boundaries between self and other.

Those who exhibit no regard for borders because of the unregulated and hurtful emotions borders evoke, often simultaneously tend to expect favor and cannot even begin to fathom that others might not want to favor them. Clinicians note this phenomenon as they explain that narcissistic personality disorder wields a "sense of entitlement, i.e., unreasonable expectations of especially favorable treatment," which is connected to a "pervasive pattern of grandiosity."[16] Not receiving what they feel entitled to they become frustrated, often using their disappointment to justify the exploitation and abuse of others. It is important to realize here that patients with narcissism are not inherently mean-spirited; more accurately, trapped by feelings of being shortchanged and victimized, they lash out at anyone who crosses their path. As they are anesthetized to the feelings of others, people with narcissism are ill-equipped to be charitable to them. Possibly like Gwen Araujo's enemies, they are not up to the emotional challenge of being about borders. Instead of respecting the differences of one another or accepting the connection with one another, they attempt to convert and even absorb anyone who is different into themselves.

---

[16] *Diagnostic and Statistical Manual of Mental Disorders (DSM-IV-TR)*, 4th ed., text rev. (Arlington, VA: American Psychiatric Association, 2000), 717.

Through clinical treatment it becomes apparent that in boasting about their grandiosity, victims of narcissism are creating a cover story—the one true story—for their genuine feelings. Behind this story and façade of superiority, those with narcissistic personality disorder have a fragile sense of self-esteem, craving constant attention and admiration in order to hold together their fantasy of personal integrity. Like Ovid's Narcissus, the pathological narcissist seeks an everlasting perfect self-image to sustain an estimation of self-worth. Not surprisingly, persons with narcissistic tendencies associate themselves with someone or someplace they consider superior in order to build themselves up, such as an expert in the medical field, a celebrity, an ivy league institution, pedigree background, or even valuable land. One's narcissistic relationship with the idealized person or place is extremely delicate to the extent that if the person or place becomes tainted for any reason, the affected person suffers from what clinicians call narcissistic injury. Any scar on the idealized other becomes a scar on the person with narcissism, rendering others only useful when they satisfy the narcissist's need for esteem. Pathological manifestations of narcissism make being open to the emotional give-and-take of every-day relations, or what I have been calling charity, nearly impossible.

Overcoming the boundary issues intrinsic to narcissism is a rigorous procedure, since the narcissist's larger-than-life self-image makes criticism particularly difficult to process. We all have experienced the need to be in the right frame of mind to accept even the most constructive of criticism. Most of us capitulate to doing so solely because we want to improve ourselves and our relationships with others. What if one cannot recognize the boundaries, the differences, between oneself and another? This is precisely the case in narcissism where emotions are to be avoided at all costs, making a bordered self inconceivable and hence any self-correction impossible.

Heinz Kohut has researched extensively the diagnosis and treatment of narcissism. He has identified various degrees of it, all of which are traceable to the affected person not being able to relinquish childhood needs.[17] People with narcissism remain stuck in an undeveloped simplistic ego in which their self-esteem is based on an idealized image of the self. For Kohut, treatment of narcissistic personality disorder depends

---

[17] For an in-depth analysis of the clinical research on narcissism, see Heinz Kohut, *The Analysis of the Self: A Systematic Approach to the Psychoanalytic Treatment of Narcissistic Personality Disorders* (New York: International Universities Press, Inc., 1971) and *The Restoration of Self* (Madison, WI: International Universities Press, Inc., 1977).

on developing three emotive and imaginative dimensions of human existence: empathy, creativity, and humor. Empathy, which is feeling for others without over-identifying with them, needs to be fostered for healing to begin and for genuine relationships to thrive. Christians can learn from clinicians as they work toward incarnating a human existence that is open to the complexity of corporeality. For believers, being human in the face of one another and in the presence of God must embrace an anthropological subject whose feelings matter to the extent that they are engaged and open to transformation.

It is worth repeating that emotional and physical neglect and abuse during one's childhood is a possible cause of narcissism. Whether the feelings of a particular childhood trauma are too painful to handle or as a result of experiencing trauma one has limited tolerance for dealing with emotions, those feelings that bring pain and shame are subverted by identifying with an ideal noncorporeal image. The other main cause of this disease takes place when parents project a label of specialness onto their child in order to support their own egos.[18] Typing one's child as special without merit could be neglectful in its own right as it fails to prepare the child to deal with life's ups and downs, to handle the positive and negative emotions associated with living with others. Sheltered from less than pleasurable affect, these children could become narcissistic adults who avoid intimate relationships and intense emotions, hiding behind a noncorporeal, idealized, privileged, godlike sense of self.

Whether due to egregious forms of trauma or to the over-coddling of a child, narcissism creates obstacles to being about borders. In the first place, people with narcissism ignore or do not realize otherness because of their unbounded sense of self. Recall that Ovid's Narcissus dies because he confuses the water with himself. Likewise those suffering from narcissism fail to realize the world as different from themselves. Like newborn babies, victims of narcissism have at the core of their psyches a projection that they are the world, rendering outside persons and intimate relationships superfluous. This is more than being self-centered in which one places the self above all others; on the contrary, it is about a failure to detect boundaries between self and other altogether. Without acknowledging borders between self and other there is no way to engage others in all their particularity. For those with this mentality, to be or not

---

[18] Alexander Lowen, *Narcissism: Denial of the True Self* (New York: Macmillan Publishing Co., 1983). Whereas Kohut focuses on diagnosis and treatment, Lowen explores the social impact of the narcissistic condition on both subject and other.

to be about borders is not even a question as they cannot locate borders in the first place. Narcissism further destroys one's capacity to be about borders as it causes its victims to disconnect from any and all feelings involving intimacy. If feelings typically motivate people, what happens to the victims of narcissism who deny all emotion? They have many options from which to choose. They can lie about, rationalize, or repress situations, people, and stories that bring about feelings that disrupt their idealized self-images. Engaging in any one of these strategies, they hope to escape the vulnerability and relationships of interdependence that accompany hybrid existence.

NARCISSISM AS SINFUL?

One might be tempted to argue that narcissists are closer to living hybrid existence than the rest of us because of their comfort with playing with boundaries, that is, allowing for their porosity. Nevertheless, incarnating hybrid existence means first and foremost one must be attentive to boundaries in order to respect the commonalities and difference that arise at them. When we fail to be vigilant about affect, and hence fail to deal with borders, we are sinning against our neighbor by refusing to realize their needs, feelings, memories, and stories. The refusal to acknowledge the humanity of the other is the brokenness in which we are all implicated and for which we are all responsible to work toward fixing, healing, and reconciling.

Some feminist theologians, including myself, resist employing the discourse of "sin" because it has been used to devalue women, starting with Eve as the locus of human transgression. One cannot adequately attend to the plurality of identity, however, without sustaining, in the words of Serene Jones, "serious reflection on the depth to which persons can 'fall' in their brokenness and their participation in the breaking of others."[19] Sin in the midst of hybrid existence occurs when we fail to attend to the needs, feelings, memories, and stories of another. We sin in this way not necessarily because we are mean-spirited or even because we are consumed totally by narcissism but perhaps, as Bernard Lonergan explains, because such sin is a result of *scotoma*, of being blinded to our hybrid existence. We experience this blindness as bias, which prevents

---

[19] Serene Jones, *Feminist Theory and Christian Theology: Cartographies of Grace* (Minneapolis: Fortress Press, 2000), 70.

us from having insights about ourselves that would reveal negative feelings toward others, such as fear, prejudice, and anger, consequently prohibiting us from acknowledging how our individual and group stories are multiple and enmeshed with those of others.[20] Overcoming the brokenness among individuals and groups that results from not engaging feelings is the first step in being about borders.

Some of us suffer from the opposite of the narcissistic effect, in that we place so much emphasis on the needs, feelings, memories, and stories of the other that we ourselves become worn away, that our borders are neglected. Here, one's own feelings need to be attended to, boundaries of self, place, and story need protection, not to the exclusion of the other, but so that one can meet the other whole and ready to participate in genuine relationships with them. If ourselves, stories, and places have been worn down to nothing, then we have no borders to be vigilant about. Self-love is an important piece to being about borders.[21] Returning to the issue of sin, it is feasible to argue that *scotoma* can unfold not only in being blind to the stories of others, but to those of one's own as well.

NARCISSISM ON THE GROUP LEVEL

Whether dealing with too much narcissism or not enough self-love, it is fair to say that how one deals with borders transcends the life of the individual, influencing group identity formation. According to Christopher Lasch, narcissism on the group level creates values that leverage groups against one another, spiraling into insidious social problems, such as sexism, antienvironmentalism, and militarism.[22] If, as in the case of the clinical disorder of narcissism, cultures and nations begin to lose perspective of where they end and another begins, then any initiative to convert or absorb the other group into the dominant one is legitimized. An assumption even emerges: what is good for us must be good for them. In the United States, where constant fears and threats about terrorism flourish in a social setting of self-importance, the cultural presentation of narcissism worsens. The narcissistic façade of superiority is transformed

---

[20] For a discussion of the four avenues by which bias occurs, see *Collected Works of Bernard Lonergan*, ed. Frederick E. Crowe and Robert Doran, vol. 3, *Insight: A Study of Human Understanding* (Toronto: University of Toronto Press, 1997), 214–20.

[21] For more on the importance of self-love, see Vacek, *Love, Human and Divine*.

[22] Christopher Lasch, *The Culture of Narcissism: American Life in an Age of Diminishing Expectations* (New York: W.W. Norton & Company, Inc., 1979).

into a struggle for survival in which many people see themselves as victims regardless of their actions. Moreover, any feeling for others at the borders is nullified by fear and desperation. In such dire circumstances, being about borders manifests itself almost always perversely in a narcissistic posture of entitlement. It appears that none of us are free from narcissism's corrupting effects. When read this way, narcissism is a pathology that all humans share to some degree; it is part of the human condition and perhaps a way of imagining original sin and the brokenness of our world. While we may not be clinically diagnosed as narcissistic, we may exhibit traits that prevent us from dealing with one another's needs, feelings, and stories.

Summary

In this chapter I sketch the trouble with borders in society today, namely that they are not easily definable and hence not always secure, giving way to all sorts of negative emotions, or at least uncomfortable ones. For being about borders to emerge, affectivity of all kinds needs to be welcomed, so that one another's stories can be heard and accounted for. In other words, in being vigilant about the emotional ambiguity of border life, humanity can become more emotionally aware of the differences related to self, other, and all the hybridized spaces in-between. I also claim, albeit implicitly, that borders are not merely therapeutic tools but affective markers that define self and other. The issue for Christians is if and how they can be converted from a stance of fear, entitlement, or numbness at borders to one that embraces the ethical responsibility needed for border life. Like in individual therapy, Christian healing and moving toward right relationships with God and others depends on recognizing the borders of self and community; furthermore, it involves having the courage, strength, and commitment not only to acknowledge borders but also to remain vigilant about them.

Chapter 2

Theological Talking Points on Border Life

It is not enough to critique the situation at the borders—the fear, the entitlement, the numbness; one must also work toward constructing a new way of living with the affective turmoil their porosity brings. The doctrines of creation and Christology provide talking points for articulating a theological anthropology that is committed to dealing with the emotional effects of difference. Talking points are conversation starters, places where one can enter into discussion, debate, and leave the door open for further reflection. I find the notion of "talking points" helpful because it avoids any sense that Christianity has the one true story regarding the contemporary challenge of living with others at the same time as it claims that Christians do in fact have a particular stake in current conversations about diversity and globalization.

Talking Points on the Doctrine of Creation

Within scriptural accounts of creation, there are two canonical stories about the beginning of creaturely existence—both of which enrich and challenge the other and contest privileging any one story about what it means to be human. According to Genesis 1, men and women are created simultaneously in God's likeness, "in the image of God he created them; male and female he created them" (Gen 1:27). For many feminists, this is the great equalizing text through which one can claim that both the male and female genders are rendered good and sacred through creation.

29

This story is often lifted up to counter any unjust power relations along gender lines in cultural and ecclesial contexts. In addition to these perspectives, when reading Genesis 1, I am struck by the idea that through creation God makes an imprint on humanity. Being created in God's image and likeness, in the *imago dei*, has the potential to drive home the claim that human beings carry the story of the divine within them. When read this way, human beings are by nature hybrid, and what's more, their hybridized identity is regarded as good in and of itself. By extension, any resistance to the goodness of our multistoried selves becomes a potential site of sin and brokenness.

There are other points in Scripture that support understanding human beings as hybrid, for example in Genesis 2. There Christians are faced with another account of border life, one in which a female is created from a male and both are encouraged to live beside one another: "So the Lord God caused a deep sleep to fall upon the man, and he slept; then he took one of his ribs and closed up its place with flesh. And the rib that the Lord God had taken from the man he made into a woman and brought her to the man" (Gen 2:21-22). Even when read metaphorically, many believers, and many of them feminist, find this story problematic, since it has been used to classify women as derivatives of men and subservient to them, concretizing a gender dualism that is already rife within Christianity and culture. What if, however, one plays with the idea that in forming from the male body, females carry within them the story of the first human who was created? This is the story about someone so lonely and incomplete that he needed another to bring authenticity to his life. Perhaps in Genesis 2 we have an alternative sense of hybridity emerging, one in which the female is created as a hybrid in that she carries the story of Adam within her. Her hybridity allows her to have empathy for him. She understands his suffering because their bodies are porous and their stories overlap through their shared embodied selves, their common "rib." In making another human from the first, God creates a hybrid being, who knows the story of the other and as such is enabled to have compassion for him in his sameness and difference. This creation narrative does not then support sexist or misogynist claims and does not concretize heterosexist and spousal imagery. Instead it highlights humanity as hybrid—that the normative way of being human is having and respecting many-storied identities. One might even add that in a way the female creature best symbolizes our plural existence because in addition to being hybridized by the image of God, she is crossed and complicated by another other's story, namely that of her partner.

In the doctrine of creation, one can detect even more talking points about what is at stake in living at the borders within hybrid existence. One can hardly ignore the repeated theme in Scripture and tradition that God creates many different species—a diversity that is interpreted as good. Connected to validating the plurality among creatures is the sacralizing of the interdependence among them. All creatures are dependent on their creator for every moment of their existence, rendering being dependent and feeling vulnerable normative. Interdependence carries over to the relation among creatures. Human beings are dependent on all the plants and animals of the earth and the earth is vulnerable to the actions of all of creation. Accepting being dependent on and vulnerable to others is an essential piece of incarnating hybridity, in that in telling our stories we have to admit our connections to and differences from one another. Contrary to rationalizing the domination of one species over another, this type of logic makes the human need for relationships sacramental. Notice that the defining characteristic of being human is a relationship of difference—one that embraces being vulnerable to the needs of another because of their close proximity to them. This is the opposite of the caricature of the narcissistic individual discussed earlier.

Finally, it is worth noting that the theological idea of "sacramentality" itself, specifically the notion of God's presence in the world, further illuminates human existence as hybrid, in that there is constant exchange between the porous borders of the sacred and the everyday. Undoubtedly, among the many Christian texts and teachings on creation there are important moments that signify that hybridity and difference are normative and authentic dimensions of being human.

Talking Points on the Person and Work of Jesus Christ

Theological convictions about the person and work of Jesus Christ also provide avenues for dealing with the ambiguity and ambivalence that porous borders create. One might begin this discussion by framing Jesus himself as a person committed to dealing with difference, as each of the gospels portray him as an *other-oriented* being, meaning someone who is consistently engaged with and transformed by the stories of others. He does not hide behind the label of the one true story; indeed, he constantly challenges labels. One only need to return to Luke's Jesus and the call for table fellowship to understand how Jesus implores his followers to open to others and their many needs, feelings, memories, and, of course, stories. Jesus embraces hybrid existence by opening to and being opened by the stories of others, by being about borders.[1]

One might go even further to emphasize Jesus as a hybrid as he himself had many stories; he was a Jew, a man, a friend, and a son. His hybridity lands him in trouble on more than a few occasions, while at other times it is cause for celebration. More often than not, the effects of his hybridity are ambiguous. Few can forget the wedding at Cana, where Mary demands that her son alleviate the wine shortage and then his resistance to her request: "When the wine gave out, the mother of Jesus said to him, 'They have no wine.' And Jesus said to her, 'Woman, what concern is that to you and to me? My hour has not yet come'" (John 2:3-4). This text can be interpreted in any number of ways, even as a rebuke of Jesus' mother's assumptions. Perhaps, however, one could read the text as Mary calling Jesus to attend to another one of his stories. Although it may not be up to her to decide when and where he intervenes, her request acknowledges that he is not merely the party guest in this context; rather, in many ways he serves in the role of the host—the one who can save it from ruin.[2] Mary points us to Jesus' hybrid identity. While most of us do not have the power to change water to wine or to save the world, we do play different roles in our lives, all of which come with particular responsibilities.

In addition to illustrating his plural identity, the gospels reveal a Jesus who is well aware that other people have varied stories, some of which need to be admitted and even relinquished for a new type of existence to emerge. Recall the gospel passage in which Jesus asks his disciples to reflect on their consciences, to decide which stories are worth living and

---

[1] For more on the connection between Jesus and borders see, Roberto S. Goizueta, "'There You Will See Him': Christianity Beyond the Frontier Myth," in *The Church as Counterculture*, ed. Michael L. Budde and Robert W. Brimlow (Albany: SUNY Press, 2000), 171–93; and Goizueta, *Caminemos con Jesús: Toward a Hispanic/Latino Theology of Accompaniment* (Maryknoll, NY: Orbis Books, 1995).

[2] In the liturgical tradition, Jesus becomes the host through ritual and memory in the sacrament of the Eucharist. In claiming that through communion, "We recognize him in those around the table, we repent our collusion and complicity in their suffering and oppression, we ask his and their forgiveness, we share the body of the Lord, we *become* the body of the Lord," M. Shawn Copeland posits the Eucharist as an event illustrative of what I am calling "incarnating hybridity," whereby solidarity has the potential to emerge through God's presence in the overlapping and intertwining stories with others. See Copeland, "Body, Race, and Being," in *Constructive Theology: A Contemporary Approach to Classical Themes*, ed. Serene Jones and Paul Lakeland (Minneapolis: Fortress Press, 2005), 115–16.

dying for, and to reevaluate their ties to their family: "Whoever loves father or mother more than me is not worthy of me; and whoever loves son or daughter more than me is not worthy of me; and whoever does not take up the cross and follow me is not worthy of me" (Matt 10:37-38). Luke's Jesus puts it plainly, "So therefore, none of you can become my disciple if you do not give up all your possessions" (Luke 14:33). The message is clear, followers of Jesus need to relinquish the stories and attachments that prevent them from doing other-oriented work, specifically those facets of their identities that obscure the needs, feelings, memories, and stories of others. In both of these biblical passages, the issue of our hybrid existence is not being debated; in fact, it is taken for granted, in that Jesus is portrayed as implicitly acknowledging and accepting that we have various demands on our lives and a plurality of stories that pull us in different directions. At the same time, he explicitly asserts that we all have a responsibility to make choices about which of the stories in our many-storied identities need to be rewritten or even jettisoned for those of another. We have to manage our hybrid identities in order for life-giving relationships with others to emerge.

There are other christological talking points essential for advancing an anthropology that seriously considers hybrid existence. Doctrinal teachings on the incarnation, for example, lay on the line quite beautifully what is at stake in engaging hybridity. Christians understand "Jesus Christ is fully human and fully divine . . . one [person] . . . existing in the two natures . . . without confusion, without change, without division, without separation."[3] One could say that through the incarnation Jesus takes on simultaneously the "spatial trajectories" of humanity and divinity in which the mysterious and the mundane live in proximity, and relationships with otherness are graced and made sacramental. Hence, it is not unreasonable to suggest that the incarnation models hybridity. It must be made plain: Jesus is not a hybrid if by employing the term hybrid one means a mixture of indistinguishable entities. If, however, one speaks about the distinctiveness of two natures in close relation to the border of one another, in hypostatic union, then one can begin to imagine Jesus as hybrid, in addition to reflect on what hybridity means for those of us trying to imitate him.[4]

---

[3] As cited in Jones and Lakeland, eds., *Constructive Theology: A Contemporary Approach to Classical Themes*, 168.

[4] For more on the theo-political implications of a hybridized "Jesus/Christ," see Kwok Pui-lan, *Postcolonial Imagination and Feminist Theology* (Louisville: Westminster John Knox Press, 2005), 171–74.

Important for my discussion here is that the hypostatic union allows for the stories of the other to live in mysterious proximity, to such an extent that the divine nature overflows into human nature, gracing and redeeming creaturely existence. This "asymmetrical" relationship with otherness provides an avenue for imagining hybridity in which there is an intimacy between divinity and humanity, which does not always allow for equal exchange between parties but for vigilance about the intimate space shared, that is, a respect for the relationship in and of itself.[5] Moreover, the proximity between the divine and human natures—this border relationship—has saving power in that all that is created is graced and redeemed. When read this way, the incarnation sacralizes difference. In reflecting on hybridized existence, we might contemplate the mystery of Jesus' hybridity, not with any fixation on locating a pure story about his divinity or about his humanity, but about being opened emotionally and spiritually by the rich interplay between the border of these two stories and how similar salvific intimate relationships of proximity manifest in our own lives.

In Jesus' death and resurrection, hybridity is made manifest again as Christians proclaim that through the cross Jesus takes on the stories of many, including those of the most stigmatized at the time: women, the sick, and the outcast. He takes them on by making them important, by decentering his own need for survival in order to secure theirs. He dies for all of humanity—not just for mine or yours, but for everyone's stories; in other words, Jesus' hybridity is shaped by the needs, feelings, memories, and stories of others. Like Jesus who takes on the stories of many, Christians are chosen to bear the other's story as their own, largely because it is theirs too. As Christians believe that Jesus becomes the one who shoulders the burden of all our histories and refuses to take shelter in any one story, in any one home, they are elected to model Jesus' humble posture by carrying the weight of many in their own hybrid selves. Finally, one even could make the theological claim that one's belief in the resurrection, at least in part, points to one's hope for all of our stories to be acknowledged, even if they have to be grossly rewritten or dispensed with in an act of reconciliation with one another.

---

[5] For a fresh look into Chalcedonian Christology and the asymmetrical relationship of the two natures of Christ, see Oliver Crisp, *Divinity and Humanity: The Incarnation Reconsidered* (Cambridge, UK: Cambridge University Press, 2007), 19.

Moving from Theology to the Everyday

In thinking through these talking points, several themes begin to emerge regarding what it takes to be about borders today. Very basically, one must gear up for the emotional resistance that engaging otherness brings. One needs to be ready for conflict, not for a violent display of power, but for being embroiled in heated encounters and debates in which one or more of the parties involved may not be emotionally satisfied. One also needs to become vulnerable to negative and uncomfortable feelings to the point of being emotionally exposed in relation to others. Conflict and exposure are integral to a culminating moment in being human, namely, that of mourning any privileged stories about one's sense of self or the other. A vital dimension of our humanity, mourning represents an ability to experience loss and eventually overcome it, creating new roads for opening to the emotional demands of hybrid existence.

Readiness for Conflict

In all of the talking points on hybridity, conflict is a theme. Not to be confused with violence, conflict points to the emotional dissonance that occurs at borders of difference before physical violence ensues. It encompasses the overwhelming feelings that those affected by narcissism will do almost anything to avoid. One can sense situations of conflict through changes in body language, including gesture, tone, and intensity of affect toward one another. As difficult as it is, in trying to live like Jesus and in being about borders, it is necessary to be vigilant about the emotional eruptions of conflict in our everyday lives because they signify the needs, feelings, memories, and stories of another.

Whereas I would go so far as to say that the biblical stories about two persons sharing one rib and about a demanding mother who confronts her son at a wedding are examples of how being connected to others brings responsibility and conflict, the tumult that Jesus' ministry triggers, as illustrated in the gospels, is plain and undeniable. Certainly in questioning the authority of the Roman Empire, Jesus welcomes conflict with the dominant and powerful groups of his time. Moreover, in challenging social norms by associating with marginalized groups throughout the empire, he invites conflict. He angers powerful individuals and groups so much so that they retaliate with violence. Analogously, as we imitate Jesus' open disposition and reach out to those who are deemed "other" in society, we risk negative responses both from our peers and from those others to whom we are attempting to be oriented in the first place. Being other-oriented in some way or another puts us at risk either emotionally or physically.

It is probably understandable why our peers might react negatively to our reaching out to others; after all, who wants to have to give up privilege and change the status quo, especially if we benefit from it? This backlash is somewhat expected. Realizing why someone in need might react negatively to our expressions of charity is potentially more complicated. Perhaps the other's negative response is an indictment of our social, that is, our political, economic, and technological, privilege. Or perhaps, memories of pain and trauma prevent others from being receptive to our gestures of emotional openness. Either way, in being about borders, the emotional conflict that ensues in such cases needs to be more than tolerated; it must be encouraged. There is a qualitative difference between toleration and encouragement. When one tolerates the disruptive gestures, tones, and changes in affect of another, one merely waits and hopes somewhat passively for the uncomfortable moment to cease. More than likely, however, unless dealt with or at least admitted, negative feelings, regardless of where they originate, will reappear. So instead of merely tolerating borders and the emotional dissonance they bring, we need to seek these uncomfortable places out—encourage them—in an effort to meet the other in all their difference and similarity.

This is all easier said than done, and, admittedly, due to the high emotional threat, some of us do not feel very other-oriented at all. Like Jesus, we may be moved by the other only after the fact, only after a conflictual meeting with them. For a closer look at how conflict creates relationship, even unwanted relationship, it might help to revisit Mark's story of the encounter between Jesus and the Syro-Phoenician woman. When this other, a foreigner, a Gentile, and a woman, "beg[s] him to cast the demon out of her daughter," Jesus responds rather uncharitably: "Let the children be fed first, for it is not fair to take the children's food and throw it to the dogs." Nonetheless, the encounter does not end there. Gearing up for conflict, she challenges Jesus to engage her otherness and need, "Sir, even the dogs under the table eat the children's crumbs," and because of her poignant response, Jesus is moved—converted even—and her daughter is healed (Mark 7:26-30). This "odd couple" represents how in the most precarious of situations conflict can create opportunities for charity and relationship.[6]

---

[6] For more on the intricacies of this relationship, see Claudia Setzer, "Three Odd Couples: Women and Men in Mark and John," in *Mariam, the Magdalen, and the Mother*, ed. Deirdre Good (Bloomington: Indiana University Press, 2005), 75–92.

The point I wish to make here is a simple one: affectively charged encounters change people. Moving from theology to practice, we can see this
dynamic unfold in our ordinary lives. As many of us have experienced,
emotions can influence major life choices, including decisions about our
partners, families, and careers. Teaching in a region as economically
diverse as New York City, I often encounter college students who struggle
with the emotional choice between profit and justice. It is easy for me to
imagine a young woman who, while commuting to her internship with
a notable prestigious financial institution, encounters a homeless woman
who seems dazed and disoriented. The student probably feels uncomfortable for a number of reasons, some of which she is able to express.
She is frightened that she could be in danger of being accosted, angry
that this person probably is an addict, and sad that this person appears
lonely and marginalized. The feelings she cannot name are the most
problematic. These are the emotions deep-seated in her that incite a need
to do something for this other human being despite the student's entire
lifestyle prohibiting such an inclination. After all, she is on her way to
an internship, a position that nurtures lucrative profit margins possibly
at the expense of others. When faced with another at the borders, the
intern experiences a conflict that implores her to choose to be for or
against the other.

Sometimes emotional conflict is far less internal and private, and can
even emerge in social situations in which the parties involved know one
another. For example, conflicts could arise at family gatherings because
the subject matter in question is too painful to engage fully, because the
tenor of the repartee is too emotionally charged, because there are too
many radically different opinions present, or even because both parties
are working with very different conversational styles.[7] Sometimes the
most debilitating forms of conflict surface in a discontinuity of affect or
gesture, when we cannot intellectually interpret or manage another's
emotional response to a situation. This can occur with those whom we
are closest, when after many years of relationship we still cannot accurately
read their feelings or gestures and instead end up making assumptions
about what their motives are. Disjunctures caused by incomprehensible
feelings or disparate forms of body language are troublesome to deal
with because the affective dissonance they create escapes concrete

[7] For an analysis of the breakdown in relationships caused by differences among
parties' conversational style, including their voice tone, pitch, and phrasing, see
Deborah Tannen, *That's Not What I Meant: How Conversation Style Makes or Breaks
Relationships* (New York: Ballantine Books, 1986).

linguistic norms. Not easily intellectualized, categorized, or understood, such bodily affect and gestures have the potential to create what Jean-François Lyotard calls a *differend*, or a situation of conflict that cannot be resolved by discourse.[8] Being vigilant about the affective ambiguity in any and all of these conflicts is a crucial move toward being about borders. As painstaking as it is, H. A. Williams reminds us that our only choice is to work through conflict: "It is when we refuse to recognize and welcome tensions which are life-giving that we fall prey to tensions which are death-dealing."[9]

Openness to Exposure

A second theme emerges in thinking through the talking points on border life—the importance of embracing vulnerability and our dependence on others. Much of the difficulty of dealing with conflict is opening oneself to all the feelings of vulnerability that accompany being human with others and being dependent on them—being emotionally exposed or naked. It takes a lot of courage and discipline to admit feeling afraid or ignorant when encountering someone who is different. Arguably, it takes even more courage to admit one's dependence on this other person. Within the doctrine of creation, nonetheless, Christians can find support for conceptualizing vulnerability and dependence as righteous and even sacramental.

As we have seen, stories about creation and human existence portray a dynamic sacramental encounter with the transcendent other who calls us into being, on whom we are dependent for every moment of our existence. In saying yes to this invitation, as with any other relationship, as creatures we must embrace being vulnerable to the unpredictable and uncontrollable dimensions of it. This means very practically, when we sense another at borders, we must not only be ready for conflict with them but also be willing to open ourselves to their mysterious particularity, with little knowledge of how the encounter ultimately will unfold. In relating to others, as exemplified by God's relating to humanity in the Garden of Eden, all bets are off. We may have intentions and even hopes for our relationships, yet finally there comes a realization that living at

---

[8] See Jean François Lyotard, *The Differend: Phrases in Dispute*, trans. Georges Van Den Abbeele (Minneapolis: University of Minnesota Press, 1988).

[9] H. A. Williams, *Tensions: Necessary Conflicts in Life and Love* (Springfield, IL: Templegate, 1977), 13.

the borders with one another involves letting go of all pretensions about knowing how things will turn out. Being about borders is a way of speaking about the affective draw of relationships without the rational payoff. As in a parent-child relationship, there is no clear way to know what choices will be made and what the outcome of those choices will be. Living in the midst of hybrid existence similarly encompasses trekking unsettled terrain with little more than being vigilant about one's feeling for others, including one's feelings of vulnerability and dependence in these uncertain relationships.

Beyond the creation narratives, and through the incarnation, Christ sacralizes human vulnerability and dependency. In becoming flesh, he wages a new path for being human—one that is open to exposure for others.[10] Moreover, as we have seen, in his other-oriented activities and risking his life for the marginalized, Jesus models the complete exposure and mysterious embrace of the human condition, embodying what it takes to be part of the new creation. In dying on the cross, Jesus Christ forever sacralizes physical and ontological limits. Finally, in his resurrection, Christ creates hope for renewed relationships, ones in which the pain and shame of brokenness are healed and reconciled in the face of God and others—in the presence of an interdependent community. In each of these dimensions of the kenotic story of Jesus Christ, including his ministry, death, and resurrection, asymmetrical relationships of dependence are rendered positive, sacramental, and salvific.

Cultural pressures distort scriptural and theological norms, and in our everyday practices exposure is rarely revered, never mind regarded as sacred. Already I have argued that the effects of narcissism numb some to emotion, rendering sensing the needs of another impossible. An inability to feel for another has further detrimental effects in that it prevents one from being vulnerable and dependent. Exposure to any raw feelings is the beginning of the end of the narcissist's idealized sense of self and only would result in an onslaught of seemingly disjointed and destructive feelings, ultimately manifesting in narcissistic injury. Instead of embracing the conflicting emotions fomenting inside of themselves, those with narcissism display a façade of independence in which all exposure is avoided. Embracing the corporeal nature of being human, including

[10] Anthony J. Godzieba locates physical vulnerability and ontological frailty as exemplified in the incarnation as pivotal themes in Catholic theology and practice, see "Incarnation, Theory, and Catholic Bodies: What Should Post-Postmodern Catholic Theology Look Like?" *Louvain Studies* 28 (2003): 217–31.

the moments of interdependence that characterize creation, is a seemingly insurmountable challenge for the victims of narcissism and a formidable task for the rest of us struggling with similar obstacles in ordinary living.

Many of us practically have been brainwashed to repudiate being dependent on others and to hide our very human fears of helplessness and failure. Everything in our lives tells us that finitude is negative and that limits are for the weak. As more products are developed to help make life easier and longer, such as medical cures and treatments, dietary pills and programs, cosmetic products like Botox, and computers and wireless technology, there seems to be less tolerance for people who cannot manage their own lives and control their embodied selves. There is no end to what limits one attempts to push and borders one tries to overcome. Recent discussions of the parameters of stem cell research also tread on questions about human limits.

My intention here is not to manufacture nostalgia for the good old days, since I wholeheartedly appreciate the abundance of inventions that improve my quality of life. Yet anyone who has dealt with someone who is chronically and critically ill senses on some level that many modern advancements need to be questioned. How much medical intervention is too much? How many operations are too many? How many rounds of rehabilitative therapy are really necessary or justifiable? At what point is one obligated to question at what cost and to whose benefit these interventions serve? Few of us ever get very far in this questioning. The affectively charged crisis moments of medical emergencies do not allow for pondering why and if we should succumb to such procedures. One response is that we are afraid of death, but our fears go deeper. We are afraid of losing our autonomy. One could make the claim that we would rather risk life itself through undergoing extreme saving procedures than chance being sick and dependent on others.

There are no clear answers to these debates surrounding quality of life and end of life issues as the Terri Schiavo case made our private confusion and anxiety about such matters plain to the public eye.[11] One may recall Schiavo, the Florida woman in her late twenties, who suffered brain damage after collapsing in her home. For almost fifteen years after, her husband and parents battled about what was to be her fate. She died

---

[11] See Joshua E. Perry, Larry R. Churchill, and Howard S. Kirshner, "The Terri Schiavo Case: Legal, Ethical, and Medical Perspectives," *Annals of Internal Medicine* 143, no. 10 (November 15, 2005): 744–48, http://www.library.manhattan.edu:2612/ (accessed August 24, 2010).

eventually after a judge ruled that she would no longer receive nutrition or hydration. Through the ongoing media coverage about her life, many ethical issues were publicly debated, including how her complete dependence on others compromised her humanity. While I am not taking sides in this very complicated case, one point seems clear in the analysis of her life and death. Human vulnerability, including dependence on others or what I have been calling exposure, is not read generally as a positive dimension of being human.

There is a long legacy of this in Western Enlightenment thought in which philosophers such as Immanuel Kant and Jean-Jacques Rousseau redefine what it means to be human from being communally oriented to being individualistic, relegating relationships of dependence to sites of weakness and of liabilities.[12] For both Kant and Rousseau the emotive ties that draw one to another prevent the subject from living up to his or her potential. With the rise of modernity, which is typified by the valorization of reason over emotion, people became socialized to not being dependent on others for help, to believe that we could control our lives and become masters of our own destiny. The upshot of this conviction is that those who continue to express a need for people are deemed vulnerable and sometimes negatively typed as aberrant and deviant. Depending on others has become construed as a sign of impotence, a disability even.

While I hope to cultivate practices in everyday existence that honor vulnerability, one must admit that there is a destructive side to exposure in that some people relish feeling vulnerable and use their feelings to rationalize unjust actions at the borders. Psychologists strive to change such behaviors in people whose perverse sense of fear in feeling threatened by others manifests in narcissistic displays of entitlement and in ethnocentric displays of nationalism, patriotism, and triumphalism.[13] This fear of others is fueled by the logic of survival in our narcissistic

[12] For more on how Kant and Rousseau interpret freedom as limited by relations of dependence, see Charles Taylor, "Kant's Theory of Freedom," in *Philosophical Papers: Volume 2, Philosophy and the Human Sciences* (Cambridge, UK: Cambridge University Press, 1985), 318–37. Interestingly, more often than not an insidious gender dualism develops from the dismissal of the affective aspect of human relations of dependence. Females become linked to the weakness associated with emotion, rendering them less worthy than their male counterparts.

[13] For more on how attitudes or "belief domains," such superiority, injustice, distrust, helplessness, and vulnerability, cause situations of conflict to foment into violence, see Judy I. Eidelson and Roy J. Eidelson, "Dangerous Ideas: Five Beliefs That Propel Groups Toward Conflict," *American Psychologist* 58, no. 3 (2003): 183.

culture that was previously mentioned—a timidity that ignores the daunting borders that mark otherness. In a world of violence, hurried lifestyle, and loneliness, we feel all too vulnerable at these borders because we seem to have no control over the circumstances. Vulnerability here functions as a mask to hide the shame of our helplessness, finitude, and humanity.

Whether fear has been construed as a weakness or a weapon for deadly actions, we have learned to avoid situations of being exposed, of acknowledging our feelings, and maintaining close relationships. Some of us have even become accustomed to distancing ourselves from those who need help and companionship. Considering theological and psychological readings of exposure, it is imperative in being about borders to envision vulnerability and dependence not in terms of shame or fear but as sacred signs of our finitude. Only in rewriting human exposure as a virtue rather than a liability can we fully become human at the borders with others in the midst of our moving and mixing with them.

Mourning the "One True Story"

In each of the theological talking points, there is a sense of having to let go of the security of oneself and one's story in order to open to that of another. Hence, the last theme in being about borders is an engagement of that loss to the extent of mourning it. As already shown, Scripture implies that being connected with others is the end of a way of being human that privileges self alone. Whether interpreting that connectedness in Genesis 2 through Adam and Eve's shared rib or conceptualizing connectedness through Jesus' other-oriented activity, Christian discipleship calls us to surrender our comforts to make room for that of another. In addition to Scripture, the incarnation functions as a symbol of surrender. In becoming human, Jesus Christ relinquishes the primacy of the one story, kenotically surrendering himself to a hybrid existence that undercuts any absolute identity, creating room for the other.[14] While this call for kenosis in our everyday existence would most definitely entail forfeiting exclusive claims to resources, land, or cultural capital, for me,

---

[14] Aware of the many theological nuances to understanding kenosis, throughout this work I employ the term rather loosely as a way of speaking about self-giving and emptying for another. For a helpful analysis of the reading of kenosis in Christology, see Crisp, *Divinity and Humanity: The Incarnation Reconsidered*, 118–53.

the aspect most neglected in theological anthropology is embracing one's intimate connections at the border through becoming undone emotionally by the other, to the point of becoming an emotional exile, which I will elaborate on later.

While the call for relinquishment is clearly part of the Christian tradition, what is missing, at least as I understand it, is a practical means to realize that this giving up comes with a loss, which must be dealt with so we can move on and reconfigure life-affirming relationships with God and others. Put another way, a place needs to be set at the table or an item needs to be put on the agenda for a process of mourning the loss of an idealized self and story. In attempting to understand Christian discipleship in terms of dealing with loss and mourning, I turned to my colleague and New Testament scholar, Claudia Setzer. She reminded me of the biblical passage about the rich young man, who asks Jesus what he needs to do to have eternal life. After a quick exchange about keeping the commandments, Jesus explains his bottom line, "'If you wish to be perfect, go, sell your possessions, and give the money to the poor, and you will have treasure in heaven; then come, follow me.' When the young man heard this word, he went away grieving, for he had many possessions" (Matt 19:21-22). I can empathize with the rich young man, not because I am rich, young, or a man, rather because giving up is hard to do; it often causes extreme grief and raises all sorts of uncomfortable feelings, such as fear, sadness, and resentment. Moreover, when the thing we are called to give up is a particular story about oneself or another, that too is difficult, that too leads to complex emotions, and that too must be mourned. We are called to grieve like the rich young man, not in a perpetual state of mourning, but in a realization of just how much things are going to change in order for something greater to be realized.

From a pragmatic perspective, dealing with loss in being about borders is at the very least a two-step process. First, it involves relinquishing feelings and stories of fear that prevent us from opening up to otherness, surrendering the sense of entitlement that we are the only ones who deserve anything at the borders, and letting go of the façade of not feeling at all because we are so ill-equipped to deal with emotion. Second, we must mourn the loss of those negative feelings and patterns, ultimately mourning the privileged singular self and story behind those feelings and patterns. Mourning grounds the process of being about borders in that it allows for the negotiation of one's feelings, self, story, and even place in relation to that of another. Mourning sets the scene for incarnating hybridity.

The affective dimensions of mourning are sometimes so painful that they become paralyzing. We have, however, no other viable options. If we want to move forward with life-giving relationships, then we need to fight through the paralysis and jettison and grieve our privileged stories about ourselves and others. For Freud, mourning is "the reaction to the loss of a loved person, or to the loss of some abstraction which has taken the place of one, such as one's country, liberty, an ideal, and so on."[15] Analogously, the loss grieved in being about borders is the loss not of another person but rather of a privileged and singular sense of self, story, or place in relation to another—one that blinds individuals and communities to the responsibilities associated with border life. If one capitulates to the claim that borders are porous and that hybrid existence is descriptive of life amid leaky boundaries, then one has no choice but to relinquish the privilege of having one pure, right, singular identity in relation to another. That could be difficult for anyone to accept, and not only may require the act of surrendering an idealized story, but also may demand a time for mourning the privilege and safety guarded by it.

Mourning in this sense becomes integral to living as Jesus did. In being about borders, Christians are called to build and sustain intimacy at the boundaries between what's ours and what's yours without any narcissistic attachment. Breaking free of narcissism and relinquishing privilege must not go unnoticed in that the privilege must be mourned in order for transformation to occur and for charity to become a lived reality. In the theological anthropology of difference that I sketch throughout this book, human beings are chosen to gear up for conflict, open to vulnerability, and mourn the loss of a righteous sense of self and story. Quite possibly, mourning is the most graceful response to the sin of holding on to the one true story at the expense of all others.

In her work on Christian spirituality's contribution to healing trauma, Teresa Rhodes McGee underscores grief and mourning as vital to creating right relationships in a world of brokenness. She explains grief as "giving way to imagination that is at the heart of transforming the traumatic experience," and argues that trauma survivors "cannot move into the future without the acknowledgement of the memory [of the traumatic

---

[15] Sigmund Freud, "Mourning and Melancholia," in *The Standard Edition of the Complete Psychological Works of Sigmund Freud*, vol. 14, trans. James Strachey (London: The Hogarth Press, 1957), 243.

event], and genuine mourning that such pain exists in the world."[16] Like those trying to bring meaning to their interrupted lives, Christians can find peace at borders by embracing the pain associated with realizing their stories of privilege, and eventually letting both the pain and the stories go. In this way, mourning becomes a sign of one's appreciation for and obligation to the tremendous burden of hybrid existence. By mourning the privilege of having the one pure and righteous story, Christians can become vigilant to Jesus' call to be about borders by embracing the other in charity or empathy. Those with empathy try to understand the predicament of others—not to overidentify with them in any narcissistic way. Empathy enhances the cognitive and moral work involved in one's relationship with another. In recent research on trauma treatment and in trauma studies, there is a considerable amount of attention to the role of empathy, and it resonates with my reading of charity as an expression of affective openness. Thus, for the remainder of this work, I use the terms "charity" and "empathy" interchangeably.

Dominick LaCapra develops a notion of empathy "in terms of attending to, even trying, in limited ways, to recapture the possibly split-off affective dimension of the experience of others. Empathy may also be seen as counteracting victimization, including self-victimization."[17] Furthermore for LaCapra, "Being responsive to the traumatic experience of others, notably of victims, implies not the appropriation of their experience, but what I would call empathic unsettlement, which should have stylistic effects or, more broadly, effects in writing which cannot be reduced to formulas or rules of method."[18] Even those of us who have not experienced trauma all too often move to limit our identity into one safe story—to one neat formula. In thinking through what it means to be about borders, Christians are challenged to resist these enticing feelings related to one's safety. If Jesus wanted to feel secure, he would not have acted out against social norms. On the contrary, his posture implores Christians today to surrender and mourn all sense of safety for that of another.

Even though LaCapra urges a posture of empathic unsettlement in writing history of and about peoples who have experienced trauma,

[16] Teresa Rhodes McGee, *Transforming Trauma: A Path toward Wholeness* (Maryknoll: Orbis Books, 2005), 89.
[17] Dominick LaCapra, *Writing History, Writing Trauma* (Baltimore: Johns Hopkins University Press, 2001), 40.
[18] Ibid., 41.

such as victims of apartheid and the Shoah, as one may have already intuited, I am proposing that Christians use this as a template for being human. In attempting to live in the image of God and in a manner that honors the person and work of Christ, similar challenges arise, including "the problem of composing narratives that neither confuse one's own voice or position with the victim's nor seek facile uplift, harmonization, or closure."[19] In being about borders, Christians must ask themselves how they ought to engage others with both distinctive and common stories. Should they pretend that there is no ambiguity, that borders are not permeable, and potentially demonize the others at the borders? Or rather because of their intimate proximity, should they ignore the borders altogether and take over, that is, appropriate the other's sense of self, story, and place? For me, the only hope for being human in the midst of hybrid existence is another strategy—waiting for otherness, being vigilant about borders, and feeling for them, even if that means mourning our secure and closed identities. The anthropological model I am suggesting is based on an affective openness to the other, working through the trauma that leads many of us as individuals and groups narcissistically to avoid the feelings around any and all borders. This new way of living requires empathy much like the type LaCapra is a proponent of, one "that resists full identification with, and appropriation of, the experience of the other."[20] It urges one to seek out what Levinas calls "affective disturbance[s]"—events that jar one on a visceral level to do something and to embrace empathic unsettlement.[21] It surrenders all hope for easy answers at borders with another and mourns that loss too.

Mourning cannot and should not be conceptualized as a negative moment in our otherwise ordinary lives of trying to live with others. Rather, it must begin to be understood as an expression of one's inestimable gift to the other grounded in one's faith in Christ. It is an important piece of our being human with others at the borders, even a graceful response to the sinful situation of *scotoma*. We all can suffer from the effects of not seeing the presence of the other's stories within ourselves. Mourning admits this oversight and struggles to see clearly. It is a grace-filled opportunity for everyone.

---

[19] Ibid., 78.

[20] Ibid., 79.

[21] Emmanuel Levinas, *Alterity and Transcendence*, trans. Michael B. Smith (New York: Columbia University Press, 1999), 26.

Not all would accept my equal opportunity offer to mourn. LaCapra is quick to point out that those who have the "right to mourn" is a debatable issue: "The broader question here is whether empathy and, even more specifically, mourning are both available to anyone and deserved by all others, regardless of subject position. For example, how can former perpetrators develop empathic relations toward former victims and be able to engage in processes of mourning for them which are not simply perfunctory or encased in hollow commemorations?"[22] Surely not everyone has to relinquish the same story and not everyone experiences hybridity the same. Nonetheless, if we take the notion of hybrid existence seriously we have no choice but to allow and even encourage everyone to engage mourning as praxis, since no one individual has any self-enclosed, pure identity that is not trespassed and changed by that of another.

Summary

Above we have begun to explore the theological implications of living at borders for humanity. While living at the borders needs to be taken literally, it cannot remain there. Being about borders also must be understood within a larger metaphorical sense, namely, that engaging in any relationship demands the admission that the other is different and that alterity influences how one thinks, acts, and, most important, feels. In a world that seems to be losing sight of boundaries and hence the implications of difference through both the processes of globalization and social narcissism, Christians are called to bear witness to borders, not with fear, entitlement, or numbness, but with an embrace of the creative conflict and the affective ambiguity they bring. The doctrines of creation and of the person and work of Jesus Christ can provide talking points for thinking about what it takes to be about borders in the midst of hybrid existence, in which conflict, exposure, and mourning become necessary ingredients for healthy border life, for living among one another with multiple and overlapping stories.

---

[22] Dominick LaCapra, *Writing History, Writing Trauma*, 214.

Chapter 3

Navigating Borders in Our Personal Lives

Few borders are more treacherous to navigate than those within our intimate relations. They challenge us to expose our most treasured stories to the other who stands concretely before us—the other in our neighborhood market, school, or home, the other we encounter on a regular basis. The emotional stakes in these border situations are high, and great care must be taken for life-giving relationships to flourish. With all this urgency, where does one begin to be about borders? One might start with the human body. Even if narcissism deludes us into thinking that we have no personal limits, the affective disturbances that materialize in our bodies when we encounter another tell us otherwise. Beyond the contours of the body, many deal with emotionally charged borders within their families. The relationship between that of a parent and a child unequivocally entails a lifelong process of dealing with porous borders and the challenges they bring. There are other opportunities to be about borders within our personal lives. When we share our most cherished stories about our cultural backgrounds with another, we have no choice but to grapple with leaky borders. Relating to others as if there is one pure true story about our ancestral origin, in other words denying our hybridity, seems dishonest if not unethical in today's pluralist world. In what follows, I explore each of these scenarios, claiming ultimately that being vigilant about the emotional effects of moving and mixing in a world with others is the most faithful way to honor creation and the person and work of Christ.

Bodily Borders

What does one mean by the terms "body" and "bodily borders"? When I speak about body here I mean very concretely the flesh that walks with us throughout life, including eyes that cannot see too well, the scars marking where one's breasts used to be, the mind that gets fuzzy with too much drink or not enough food. I do not portend to mean the mass of flesh over which one strives to have total control; rather, following the lead of Stephanie Paulsell, I read the body as the potential border "that allows us to reach out for one another" in both positive and negative ways.[1] The body is the site of our intimate and distant relations with others, and, as such, if one hopes to invite difference into his or her life, one must be vigilant about the emotional reactions experienced both in relation to another's body and to the limits of his or her own.

The Power of Touch

One of the many ways we reveal stories about our bodily borders is through touch. Of particular theological significance, Jesus is illustrated in the gospels as an other-oriented person who uses bodily contact as a way of creating solidarity with the marginalized in his society. Those in the Christian tradition are well-versed in the stories about Jesus inviting the sick and outcast into relationship and community through corporeal encounter, including those related to his healing a leper through touch (Mark 1:40-41; Matt 8:1-3; and Luke 5:12-13). Breaking with social convention, in reaching out to others, Jesus risks his personal safety for the benefit of the other. Stories about his bodily engagements are so important for Christians that they are mimicked in various hagiographies. One of the most notable in the Catholic imagination is St. Francis of Assisi who is portrayed as having nursed the sores of the sick and the poor in medieval Europe. In a piece of modern hagiography on St. Francis, Donald Spoto writes: "With no money to give and no food to share—for he, too, was now reduced to begging—Francis knelt down and gave what he could: an embrace, a bit of comfort, a few sympathetic words. Francis would almost certainly have remembered the New Testament accounts in which Jesus healed a leper. 'Moved with pity, Jesus stretched out his hand and touched him,' which must have shocked bystanders

---

[1] Stephanie Paulsell, *Honoring the Body: Meditations on a Christian Practice* (San Francisco: Jossey-Bass, 2002), 20.

as much as the cure itself did."[2] Christians have institutionalized these stories about physical care by incorporating them into sacramental rituals, including baptism and, for Catholics in particular, anointing the sick. In our everyday practices, many of us touch one another without thinking about the theological implications. When we hug a child who needs comforting or we hold the hand of someone near death, we are being about bodily borders—making a physical connection for the sake of the other.

Not all touch is comforting or sacred, and in Catholic parish settings it would be irresponsible to emphasize the sacramental aspects of touch, especially for those who have been sexually abused by the people they trusted the most. Their stories about touch have a different ending. Unlike the child or the sick individual being consoled by touch, there are those who have not been fortunate enough to find another person's caress pleasurable. For them, bodily encounter presents as a violation and is the site of pain, shame, and perhaps trauma. When we touch one another we must be cognizant that we are engaging in acts of power and that not everyone involved has equal access to power; in other words, a specific type of bodily encounter might not mean the same for everyone involved. In probing our stories about touching in relation to advancing a type of being about borders, questions such as these arise. Does all touching reveal itself as charitable and hence empathetic? Is trespassing the borders of self and other by way of touch sacred or profane? Elected to model Jesus' border activities, Christians in particular are burdened by the issues of bodily trespass and are called not only to detect borders but also to understand how they are working and who they are benefiting—to respect and manage them.

The answers to these questions are not readily evident as we rarely have one experience or one story that we bring to our corporeal encounter with another. In hybrid existence, like ourselves, the others we touch also have a plurality of stories, making an initiative for bodily contact a precarious situation. Even though chancing physical contact in this multistoried context is dangerous because one can rarely know for sure how their gesture will be received, the answer is not to avoid all bodily contact but to pay attention to the emotional fallout of each interaction and even to be open to the possibility that one's reaction to another might change

[2] Donald Spoto, *Reluctant Saint: The Life of Francis of Assisi* (New York: Viking Compass, 2002), 58.

with time. Most bodily border situations involve tense moments of conflict, embarrassing moments of exposure, and, at times, surrendering any one right way of being present to another's needs, feelings, memories, and stories. As a result, few bodily border situations are easily categorized as positive or negative, charitable or entitled, and in being about borders, tolerating this ambiguity can be the most empathetic thing one can do. For example, a physician who hugs his or her terminally ill patient, when everything in his or her being or code of ethics goes against it, represents an embodied risk necessary in everyday life, an instance of being about borders. Embracing ambiguity in our interpersonal, corporeal relationships is a way of being open to the other and chancing the negative repercussions of border life in order for more genuine and life-giving relationships with one another to unfold.

Pushing Bodily Limits

The exploding areas of body modification and biotechnology contest notions of stable and fixed bodily borders at every turn, creating an urgent need for vigilance about the emotional dissonance of engaging difference. In both of these areas, consumerism complicates even thinking about a notion of bodily borders or limits, and, as a result, ordinary people find themselves struggling with the effects of narcissism, sometimes going to great lengths to expand, adorn, and heal themselves, all in an effort to avoid bodily limits.[3] With the rise of infomercials, shopping networks, and internet sales, the message is clear: if one acquires enough stuff, one should be happy. Furthermore, it appears that consumption is more than integral to one's happiness; it norms human existence. Arguably, authentic being in capitalistic culture is related to one's capacity for purchasing and hoarding "stuff," giving rise to an "I shop therefore I am" mentality, which has become memorialized in photography by the American feminist artist Barbara Kruger. The things we consume, including clothes, jewelry, food, real estate, and even people (children, slaves, and sexual partners), have the potential to become extensions of our body, making bodily borders anachronistic as there

---

[3] For a fascinating analysis of the connections between narcissism and body modification, including the practices of tattooing, piercing, and self-mutilation, see Kim Hewitt, *Mutilating the Body: Identity in Blood and Ink* (Bowling Green, OH: Bowling Green State University Popular Press, 1997).

seem to be no limits to self.[4] We trespass our interpersonal limits not out of malice, rather because of our deep-seated conviction that we deserve the things in question. There seems to be no end to what we need and deserve, wanting and consuming to the point at which we unwittingly open the door to a narcissistic sense of self. Globalization has hastened these effects, rendering no border insurmountable, as one can imagine having everything from hair replacements to artificial organs to surrogate pregnancies, and yet the poor still cannot escape violence, hunger, and inadequate health treatment.[5]

I have already alluded to the extreming of culture, such as body make-overs that transform one's image without heeding limits and erase all deviance from perfection. My reflections are not to ignore the place in human existence for body modification or technology, but rather to bring to light that in being about borders one is chosen to discern if and how these practices are wedded to the story that sameness is synonymous with goodness or godliness. In being about borders, one needs to do more than accept the commonsense logic that nobody is perfect and move further to mourn the feelings and attitudes related to one true story about what it means to be human, that of being safe, untouchable, perfect, and having pristine borders.

Gains in biotechnology fuel humanity's refusal of bodily boundaries. One can exist on a ventilator or can live with kidney dialysis for extended periods of time. Interestingly, people are less apt to be critical of these procedures in comparison to the cosmetic ones because medical treat-

---

[4] The chattel slavery inaugurated with the dawn of European conquest and exploration may be over; nevertheless, there is still evidence of slavery or forced labor in the United States. See Terry Coonan and Robin Thompson, "Ancient Evil, Modern Face: The Fight Against Human Trafficking," *Georgetown Journal of International Affairs* 6, no. 1 (January 1, 2005): 43–51, http://www.library.manhattan.edu:2612/ (accessed August 24, 2010).

[5] New reproductive technologies, stem cell research, and life-support systems are challenging the ways in which we think about our bodies as closed, un-transgressed entities. See Margrit Shildrick, *Leaky Bodies and Boundaries: Feminism, Postmodernism, and (Bio)ethics* (London: Routledge, 1997). The research on locating the boundaries of the human embodied self goes even further than questioning reproductive technologies to reflecting on cyborg identities. For a feminist overview of the futuristic implications of the slippery border between humanity and technology in popular culture and the media, see Jenny Wolmark, ed., *Cybersexualities: A Reader on Feminist Theory, Cyborgs, and Cyberspace* (Edinburgh: Edinburgh University Press, 1999); and for what has quickly become a classic on boundary issues, see Donna Haraway, *Simians, Cyborgs, and Women: The Reinvention of Nature* (New York: Routledge, 1991).

ments are perceived as more necessary. Yet both have the positive potential to improve the quality of a person's life and the negative potential to avoid dealing with limits and, hence, with difference. Similar to the dilemma over how much consumption is too much, questions arise here over which procedures are necessary and how they are justified as so. Which procedures are motivated by charity and which by entitlement? Again, the issue for Christians being presented in this book is not necessarily related to the ethical implications of each procedure but rather about the importance of the feelings that drive one's desire to avoid bodily finitude, and how the failure to wrestle with those emotions and the borders to which they point poses harmful physical, emotional, and spiritual consequences.

Whether deciding how or if to touch another, to alter one's body, or even to consent to the latest medical treatment, Christians are called to a new type of existence—one that embraces the emotional uneasiness of border life, including the limits of self, the proximity of the other, and all the ambiguous and emotionally volatile places in-between. In honoring both creation and the person and work of Christ, Christians are chosen to embrace the multiple stories within their corporeal identities: they are invited to incarnate hybridity. By "incarnating hybridity" I mean accepting the mysterious enmeshed nature of individual and communal life and being vigilant about the emotional dissonance that unfolds at the borders, especially the really porous and ambiguous ones, all in an effort to be responsible to the other and allow for their self, story, and place at the border to be respected.

Maternity as an Exercise in Incarnating Hybridity

While dealing with aspects of touching and the latest body procedures certainly gets at the thorny business of being about borders, I concretely incarnated hybridity when I was pregnant with my two children in a way that was unlike any other embodied interpersonal encounter of my life. During those times, feeling hostage to the other and challenged by the multiplicity of stories that informed my identity and complicated my relationships with others took on a whole new meaning. During pregnancy, it was my experience that we are chosen by the other to deal with the emotional upheaval that relationships of difference bring.

Finding out one is expecting can be the most joyous moment of a woman's life, especially if she has wanted a baby for what feels like forever. For others, discovering that they are pregnant brings a sense of dread. The pregnancy may have resulted from an incident of sexual assault or ongoing abuse. Far less toxic a situation, the woman simply may not have hoped for any or anymore children. Perhaps she has no resources to feed, clothe, and provide shelter for a child, or maybe she has been plagued by miscarriages and cannot bear another disappointment. Elation and despair are two extreme reactions to the news that one is pregnant, and arguably more than a few women find themselves somewhere in the middle, dealing with a mix of powerful emotions including excitement, happiness, anxiety, and sadness. It is not uncommon that in the midst of being hopeful for the future birth of her child, the pregnant woman cannot help resent feeling hostage to the otherness to which she is tied because somehow this other is encroaching on her understanding of self, story, and place, thereby sensing the tremendous gravity of hybrid existence.

OVERCOMING THE "ONE TRUE STORY" ABOUT MOTHERHOOD

Admitting conflicting feelings about becoming a mother is not easy. In the "developed nations," there is a widely accepted script about being a mother, one in which a woman revels in the news of being pregnant, delights in each of her trimesters, and is ecstatic about parenting this child for the rest of their life together. Questioning and rewriting this script is risky because it requires exposing oneself to feeling vulnerable and getting into conflict with oneself and others. It demands acknowledging that disparate feelings are based on a multiplicity of stories about being a mother, thereby forcing one to mourn any one pure story about motherhood.

Growing up, I always resented my own mother for telling stories about how horrible her pregnancies were. I can remember hearing about her nausea, weight gain, and fatigue, and thinking how my experience and attitude was going to be different—after all, isn't motherhood supposed to be wonderful? Particularly difficult to deal with was the negative emotion around her storytelling; it was unnerving and seemingly so "unnatural." The tenor of her emotion was so strong that it seemed to suck the air right out of the room. There was no space in her stories for the usual retorts of children being a blessing, not to mention ones of pregnant women having a glow. I remember wondering if there was something deviant or even blasphemous about my mother's sentiments.

What I know now is that my mother was expressing almost defiantly the underside of maternity, or at least shouting about the ambivalence of it. Then and now, however, "ambivalence" about maternity "remains a taboo subject."[6] It is not as if women, including theorists, theologians, and ethicists, do not express mixed emotions about conception, pregnancy, and parenting; rather, it is tough for them and others to hear. Many cringed when Adrienne Rich used the term "monstrous" to describe her experience of motherhood in the feminist classic, *Of Woman Born: Motherhood as Experience and Institution.*[7] As shocking as her language is, if we fail to acknowledge what she reveals as the negative implications of motherhood, we cannot accept the changes to identity that progeny brings. The "murderous anger" that Rich's mother sometimes experiences is all too aware of borders, the limits imposed on her, and the responsibilities lurking in this new state of being.[8] For Rich, it is not that everything about mothering is horrible but rather that everything about motherhood is ambiguous: "The bad and the good moments are inseparable for me. I recall the times when, suckling each of my children, I saw his eyes open full to mine, and realized each one of us was fastened to the other, not only by mouth and breast, but through mutual gaze."[9] This snapshot of the intricate interdependence of maternity parallels the multitude of complexities that hybridity brings into today's global world.

Positing maternity as a metaphor for what is at stake in incarnating hybrid existence creates the possibility for living with the leaky effects

---

[6] Christina Baker Kline, "Introduction," in *Child of Mine: Writers Talk about the First Year of Motherhood*, ed. Christina Baker Kline (New York: Hyperion, 1997), 6.

[7] Adrienne Rich, *Of Woman Born: Motherhood as Experience and Institution* (New York: Bantam Books, 1976), 3. Her work undoubtedly has influenced countless others. Jewish feminist theologian Judith Plaskow outlines the complicated experience of motherhood in her early work; see "Woman as Body: Motherhood and Dualism," *Anima* 8, no. 1 (Fall 1981): 56–67. Working out of a concern for ethics and public policy, Sara Ruddick posits motherhood and maternal thinking as strategies for ethical being; see *Maternal Thinking: Toward a Politics of Peace* (Boston: Beacon Press, 1989). There she claims that anyone (not just mothers and not all mothers) can learn how to use maternal thinking for community building and peace. From a contemporary continental theoretical perspective, Julia Kristeva approaches motherhood as a way of interpreting difference; see "Stabat Mater," in *Tales of Love*, trans. Leon S. Roudiez (New York: Columbia University Press, 1987), 234–63; and "Motherhood According to Giovanni Bellini," in *Desire in Language: A Semiotic Approach to Literature and Art*, ed. Leon S. Roudiez, trans. Thomas Gora, Alice Jardine, and Leon S. Roudiez (New York: Columbia University Press, 1980), 237–70.

[8] Rich, *Of Woman Born*, 5.

[9] Ibid., 12.

of otherness. Furthermore, it challenges any one true story about mother-hood, including the narcissistic projection that esteems an idealized mother with an unending reservoir of love, who sacrifices without complaint, and never loses her temper. In Roman Catholicism this perfect mother is described in spousal, heterosexist imagery in which Mary is cast as the virgin/mother, an impossible role model.[10] Such gender typing renders individuals in the church and the world, both men and women, trapped in the roles in which they have been violently cast. This "magical thinking" about motherhood has to be seriously questioned and eventually replaced with a hybrid mode of existence modeled by the cyborg woman.[11] The cyborg woman as mother carries a fetus, all the while feeling sick and tired, at times even perplexed as to how she found herself in this situation. Her feelings do not end there as she may even empathize with women who have no choice or leisure time to ponder such questions. When reading maternity as a model for living with others at the borders, one must open to the notion that the border between a woman and a fetus is far from obvious; it is porous, creating a hybrid situation that is analogous to dealing with those who are different from us in our everyday situations. Like being a mother, being human in the midst of others is "complex and profound and terrifying."[12]

Maternity is a model for being human in that it gives rise to moments that call the woman to admit to her own and another's conflicting stories about motherhood, to engage the other's stories with all the intensity and vulnerability of emotion that accompanies border life, and to mourn the idea that there is one right way to be a mother or the idea that motherhood is fundamental to her life at all. This call for mourning transcends the life stories of those persons traditionally associated with maternity

---

[10] This romanticized notion of mother can be found in the work of the Swiss theologian Hans Urs von Balthasar, among others; see von Balthasar, "Woman's Answer," in *Theo-Drama: Theological Dramatic Theory*, vol. 3, *The Dramatis Personae: The Person in Christ*, trans. Graham Harrison (San Francisco: Ignatius Press, 1992), 283–360; and "The All-embracing Motherhood of the Church," in *The Office of Peter and the Structure of the Church*, trans. Andrée Emery (San Francisco: Ignatius Press, 1986), 183–225. For a comprehensive critique of Balthasar's Marian theology, including his understanding of sexual difference, see Tina Beattie, *God's Mother, Eve's Advocate: A Marian Narrative of Women's Salvation* (London: Continuum, 2002).

[11] For more on the magical thinking about reproduction and its connection to hybrid identity, see Anne Balsamo, *Technologies of the Body: Reading Cyborg Women* (Durham, NC: Duke University Press, 1996), 80.

[12] Kline, "Introduction," 3.

and motherhood, extending to all human beings. Mourning is an undoing of the primacy of the one feeling, memory, or story about one's identity, not merely letting it go, but giving way to the uncomfortable sensation of letting it go, being open to the situation in which one might be judged for having such seemingly hostile or inhuman reactions, and grieving the idea of having one original acceptable story or script.

We all have heard these scripts or uttered them ourselves. *She should realize how "lucky" she is to be pregnant when so many others are not able to conceive. She should be "thankful" for a healthy baby.* While these everyday sayings certainly have their place, they can end up muting the important affective moments for the woman and the community, prophetic moments that signal the challenge of being emotionally and physically out of control, of living at the borders. Similar "one true story" sentiments need to be challenged or at the very least reflected on in a Christian landscape as well, such is the one true story about salvation or the one true story about what it means to be "Christian" or "Catholic."

Contrary to so much of the commonsense logic around maternity as the paradigmatic moment of creation, Rich frames motherhood as a "state of uncreation." She writes: "Most of the literature on infant care and psychology has assumed that the process toward individuation is essentially the child's *drama*, played out against and with a parent or parents who are for better or worse givens. Nothing could have prepared me for the realization that I *was* a mother, one of those givens, when I knew I was still in a state of uncreation myself."[13] Women are uncreated in maternity in that everything they thought about themselves and others is called into question as their borders are in process. Christians could and should make analogous claims about the positive undoing that emerges in trying to live with others in the image of God and in light of the incarnation.

BODILY BORDERS IN PREGNANCY

In addition to highlighting the multiple stories about motherhood, maternity also underscores the physical and emotional effects of an intense relationship of proximity with another in which both parties are constantly changing in relation to the other. Julia Kristeva writes of this disorienting process: "Cells fuse, split, and proliferate; volumes grow,

---

[13] Rich, *Of Woman Born*, 17.

tissues stretch, and body fluids change rhythm, speeding up or slowing down. Within the body, growing as a graft, indomitable there is an other. And no one is present, within that simultaneously dual and alien space, to signify what is going on. 'It happens, but I'm not there.' 'I cannot realize it, but it goes on.' Motherhood's impossible syllogism."[14] Physical symptoms of nausea, vomiting, fatigue, and fetal movement, commonly referred to as quickening, concretize this unsettling corporeal relationship with the other. When I was expecting my first child, feeling him "kick" for the first time was so exhilarating as each movement symbolized another dream that I had for his future. With my second child, there was a strange apprehension that accompanied quickening. Each poke and hiccup reminded me of my last pregnancy and that I was becoming enmeshed with that of another's story over which I had very little control. These physical changes had an emotional impact, causing fear and anxiety, not just about the health of my daughter-to-be, but about my relationship with her. Will I love this child? Will she love me? How will this new relationship and my new stories affect my other relationships?

One might think birth, which unfolds as an undeniable act of separation, clears up the physical and emotional confusion that intimate and even porous borders between mother and child bring. Nonetheless, their identities remain enmeshed, for when a lactating mother's baby cries, her breasts often fill with milk. Interestingly, even here in the most ordinary of interpersonal relations something extraordinary occurs. Emotional stimuli create a relationship of proximity, a border situation. Separation on the emotional level is never really possible when everyday life is shaped by feelings, memories, and stories related to another. A woman's story is indelibly marked by the embodied otherness that is part of her either for a short while or for a full nine months five times over.

Tracing the matrix of connections among emotions, stories, and borders through the metaphor of maternity resonates with Jesus' intimate and tenuous relations with others illustrated in the gospel traditions and emphasizes the mystery of the divinity of Jesus, specifically of God dwelling within a human being. Through the incarnation Jesus takes on humanity and divinity, representing a sort of hybrid identity, underscoring the places where the mysterious and the mundane live in proximity. Pregnancy replicates this christological tension with otherness. Accord-

---

[14] Kristeva, "Motherhood According to Giovanni Bellini," 237.

ing to Kristeva, women "live at the border, [and are] crossroad beings," and a "mother is a continuous separation, a division of the very flesh." [15] The divinity of Jesus can be imagined as known through the proximity, the anticipation, the hope, and the fear—the awesomeness—of the border between God and humanity. Even as the border is not immediately clear and separate, the intuition and feelings that point to it are evidence of mysterious otherness.

To make the hybrid existence of maternity even more complicated, there is a public quality to this very personal process of expectancy. From the very first moments of having a swollen belly others are implicated, revealing the social impact of hybrid existence. Pregnancy, according to Lilian Calles Barger, "is a period of intensified vulnerability and sensing her interconnectedness with humanity—literally. Everybody is interested; even a perfect stranger in a grocery store aisle won't refrain from commenting on her swollen belly." [16] Others who have never met the pregnant woman feel connected to her, resulting in more stories and more relations. Whether there is a "strong effect" or a "vague awareness" between the fetus and mother, the "leaky boundary" between them and the world that encounters them creates a situation that is as close as humans can get to living hybrid existence concretely. [17] If one begins to intuit the magnitude of hybrid existence, one realizes the gravity of being interconnected with others and making responsible decisions accordingly. This does not necessarily demand accepting the other automatically at all. Instead, it entails embracing a multitude of stories some of which overlap and intertwine with one another, and mourning any attachment to one story which excludes that of another. By highlighting the complexity of maternity, a more honest picture of women's experience can emerge, a portrait that might actually reflect that the more Christian thing to do for some is to not be mothers at all. Whatever the end result, as feminists continue to find space to claim the "messiness" of maternity and be heard in all their cacophony, Christians need to make a space to realize similar corporeal challenges in relating with others. [18]

[15] Kristeva, "Stabat Mater," 254.

[16] Lilian Calles Barger, *Eve's Revenge: Women and a Spirituality of the Body* (Grand Rapids, MI: Brazos Press, 2003), 75.

[17] Cristina Mazzoni, *Maternal Impressions: Pregnancy and Childbirth in Literature and Theory* (Ithaca, NY: Cornell University Press, 2002), ix, 206.

[18] Bonnie J. Miller-McLemore, *Also a Mother: Work and Family as Theological Dilemma* (Nashville, TN: Abingdon Press, 1994), 136.

Borders between Parents and Children

Imagining being about borders in the midst of hybrid existence extends beyond bodily borders into the lifelong endeavor of parenting. Clinicians argue that helping children to acknowledge, respect, and manage borders from a young age can empower them to develop life-giving relationships, some of which they may carry with them throughout their lives. Insisting on boundaries within one's relationship with one's own child, however, seems counterintuitive. Why would anyone become a parent, sometimes enduring invasive and expensive fertility treatments and even muddling through the legal quagmire of adoption, only to end up creating and enforcing a barrier with their son or daughter? Unfortunately, there seem to be few other life-affirming options, in that by refusing to be about borders within one's family, a parent risks falling victim to narcissism and breeding it in one of the most significant aspects of their lives.

Playing the Role of the Parent

It might help to begin the discussion with a hypothetical situation, one in which a parent does not want to be in the role of the "bad guy," opting instead to be his child's friend. In such a scenario a father might overhear his teenage son bragging to his friends about his sexual escapades. As a concerned parent he plans to bring up the topic of his son's emerging sexuality at dinner. Just as he is about to broach the subject, his son brings up a fond memory, and they have an easy lighthearted exchange about it. Fearing that a serious discussion might negatively affect the ease of their conversation, the concerned parent refrains from bringing up the "touchy" subject, perhaps relating to his son more like a friend than a parent. Most of us would be empathetic to the father, understanding how he might not want to push his son into a potentially threatening conversation. Still, the everyday practice of parenting calls one to acknowledge, respect, and manage the differences between being a parent and being a child.

There are reasons for ignoring borders in parent/child relationships. Some clinicians argue that many parents are afraid of making the same mistakes that their parents made and hence allow their own family systems to be organized by their children. These shifts of power within the family are supposed to give one's progeny a sense of self-esteem and confidence that they may have lacked as a child, but this strategy could be problematic as well. In being about borders in terms of parenting, it may be the case that parents have to avoid clinging to "the one true story" of being the victim of their childhood as it potentially could lead to a new child-centered story, one that blurs the boundaries between self and other to the extent that the total world becomes the domain of the child and all that is other is marginalized and even erased. Such parenting encourages children to believe that they are so special that they become unable to recognize the talents and needs of others. One could imagine a pattern of entitlement developing for both the parent and child to keep this myth of specialness viable, posing a problem for both the family and the larger society.

In *Spoiling Childhood*, Diane Ehrensaft elucidates the downside of over-indulging one's children.[19] Many have heard the theories about how too many toys or too much attention can send the wrong messages to a child, making them self-centered and difficult to be around, turning them into a wild child. Beyond this childhood Jekyll-and-Hyde myth, Ehrensaft underscores a deeper paradoxical problem in the culture of child rearing today: the self-indulgent/overindulgent parent. These parents aim for it all—a career, financial stability, life-giving relationships, and happy children, but resist having their lives changed by having children. This portrait may seem unforgiving, after all who does not want it all at some time in their life or another? I have on more than a few occasions found myself in this sticky situation, becoming self-indulgent in my desire for my life to stay the same and for me to stay the center of things even though in reality things have radically changed with the birth of my children. Self-indulgence has other implications as well, according to Ehrensaft, specifically that parents are not ready to give up being the child and refuse to be recognized as an authority figure. As an alternative they want to be loved and equate the love of the child with allowing the child to set boundaries. This is where the overindulgent element of the paradox emerges. So frustrated by their own childhood, many of which were plagued by tyrannical parenting approaches that often led to low self-esteem, parents today overcompensate by avoiding being the person in charge, coddling and building up their children to their own expense. Parents are at the same time self-indulgent with themselves and over-indulgent with their children.

---

[19] Diane Ehrensaft, *Spoiling Childhood: How Well-Meaning Parents Are Giving Children Too Much—But Not What They Need* (New York: The Guilford Press, 1997).

There are varying degrees of this problem, and while we may detect traces of ourselves in this discussion, not all coddling is pathological. Most parents tend to go through a period of parental narcissism in which they look to their children for a sense of self-worth. Nevertheless, with typical development through a process of mirroring, the child is empowered to develop a sense of self as other from the parent. This process is only successful if the parent accepts the role of the adult—of a separate entity. In a world of border trouble, it is easy to see how mirroring becomes thwarted by the parent's narcissistic, self-indulgent need to feel loved. This need is fulfilled not by a process of proper mirroring necessary for mental health development but by overindulging, coddling, and even beguiling children into thinking that they are superior at whatever they do. For Ehrensaft, it is no surprise that today children are being raised with a sense that they are special in all aspects of their lives. This form of parenting, which allows parental narcissism to continue for an unhealthy period, has negative consequences both for the child and society. It could lead to a "noncompetitive award system" in which everyone is regarded as possessing above-average talent and intellect, and according to Ehrensaft, could stall the developmental process in which the child is encouraged to cultivate their own desires and talents.[20] Likewise, extreme coaching and coddling of children may lead to an attitude of entitlement in that children are trained to think they deserve accolades, even if their behavior is less than adequate.[21]

Much of this "spoiling" unfolds in the most ordinary of settings, even at a T-ball game, a sport in which youngsters, generally four to eight years old, take turns hitting a ball off a batting tee set at home plate, abiding by rules that are parallel to the sport of baseball. After my neighbor's son returned from one such game, I asked him who had won. He replied that both teams had won, and his mother further elaborated that in her son's games no one team wins. She was quite convincing about how wonderful this all is in that every child feels good about their playing, which in turn enables them to build their self-esteem. Pushing Ehrensaft's argument one wonders if the children or the parents feel this way? Whose self-esteem is this noncompetitive game protecting? Perhaps T-ball represents the first basic level in a developmental process involving teamwork, and my analysis is over the top. Still, it is worth consider-

[20] Ibid., 125.
[21] Ibid., 122.

ing the possibility that if the child continues to be sheltered from knowledge about limits they could end up stricken by the detrimental effects of narcissism. When is the right time to begin to deal with limits that are basic to human existence? When are we mature enough to become comfortable with the life of vulnerability to which we are called?

One could pose similar questions about facing the limits regarding one's attitude toward grades throughout all levels of education. With all the conversation about grade inflation today, it is difficult to ignore how so many students think they deserve an A grade on the basis of their attendance to class and completion of assignments, rather than on the merit of their work. It is not as if the instructor is a hopeless victim in this situation; teachers can play the role of the authority figure. They can grade with attentiveness to difference, with vigilance to the boundaries in relation to academic achievement. Yet, as anyone who has ever been a teacher knows, it is tempting to avoid these sorts of academic boundaries in order to maintain one's popularity. Resisting that urge, teachers, like parents, have an opportunity to help students recognize limits and embrace the conflicts of life, even if that means being realistic about their students' distinct challenges, academic or otherwise. Arguably, it takes great courage and risk to engage the other as different, especially when that other is a child who serves as a mirror of oneself. Nevertheless, this is the journey for which we are chosen, as the only other option is spoiling children or neglecting their development. Creaturely limits and radical dependence are basic values in theological anthropology, and any acceptance of the limits of self, other, and all the spaces in-between hinges on being vigilant about borders, acknowledging, respecting, and managing them.

The Emotional Risk of Border Patrol

When parents decide to firm up the boundaries with their child, in all likelihood there will be emotional repercussions; for example, the child may become frustrated and angry. This is frightening to many adults, myself included, who do not want to make the mistakes their parents made related to punitive child-rearing strategies. The answer for Ehrensaft is not returning to those former parenting styles but rather learning to become comfortable with setting limits for one's children and being open to the emotional onslaught that most likely will emerge in the midst of the limit setting, including one's child "hating" them or thinking they are the worst parent in the world, as well as the parent feeling like a total failure and out of control. Denying that volatile affective aspect of being human in relationships by ignoring the boundaries is only a short-term fix and may cause worse feelings of negativity to fester, escalating to violence, or even the imagination of violence. Ehrensaft worries about the backlash against aggression in parenting, arguing that children who never have to deal with anger or conflict sometimes imagine anger worse than it is. An affective disturbance of any kind becomes a monster to be avoided, taking on a life of its own in the child's imagination. Children fear anger as the "great danger . . . lurking" behind the parent's façade—a violence so unspeakable, veritably unutterable.[22] This imagined fear prevents them from engaging in genuine relationships with all types of people throughout their lives.

What is so bad about getting angry, about admitting resentment, and about marking difference? How are genuine relationships with others possible without anger? In order to live as Jesus did, with charity and not with entitlement, one must realize that in the midst of our overlapping and intertwining stories, or what I have been calling hybrid existence, some borders need to be maintained so life-giving relationships can unfold. This is the challenge of being at the table with others. It is realizing how each relationship and hence each border is unique and dealing with it accordingly. The way one engages a friend may not be the best for the way one engages a child.

This type of vigilance about borders entails an openness to difference through accepting the positive and negative emotions of being in relationships with others, risking losing the short-term gain of one's affection in exchange for the long-term payoff of commitment. Being about borders in this way emulates the risk taking already alluded to in regard to the other-oriented style of Jesus of the gospels. Moreover, this mode of vigilance resonates with the theology of the incarnation in that it respects difference in the midst of intense relationships, practically sacralizing intimacy. While it may be unrealistic to think that in the heat of the moment any parent is going to reflect on these theological talking points, it helps to realize that negotiating difference in whatever aspect of our lives cannot be avoided. Being about borders seems to be a primal obligation, and definitely a Christian one.

---

[22] Ibid., 194.

Cultural Crossings

Growing up on Long Island, New York, and now working in the Bronx, New York City, I am quite comfortable with people asking me about my ethnicity. I am a citizen of the United States and my background is Italian American. While I may have conflicting feelings about my origins, I do not have a problem with the line of questioning. Such repartee invokes an intimacy among New Yorkers and creates for many a measured sense of comfort with diversity. Between my childhood on Long Island and returning to New York City as an adult, I have resided in a variety of locales, none of which have mirrored that same comfort level with inquiring into people's origins. I remember finding people's resistance to speaking about their background as off-putting and recall wondering what was at stake in my attachment to my own, especially because intellectually I know that we are living in a world in which the boundaries of ethnicities are becoming more fluid and malleable. Questions such as these absorbed me: Will anyone still be able to hold on to their ethnic story? What types of people want to? What, if any, are the ethical and theological issues here?

As these matters continued to haunt me, I began to explore them more deliberately in both my personal and professional life. I pursued them with a friend of mine who was born in Germany and had lived in London for a number of years before moving to the United States. She was a wonderful dialogue partner and unwittingly helped me write a paper on cultural hybridity for a local academic conference. During one of our conversations we discussed the reasons why some people long to identify with a certain story or place. She reminded me that others have the opposite desire, and relative to her experience, she explained how many Germans of her generation, her friends even, avoid identifying with their homeland because of the atrocities caused by the Nazi regime. They prefer to be homeless in a metaphorical sense rather than deal with their painful and shameful legacy and bear the burdens of Germany's story. The reality is that most of us would not choose to be homeless because few desire to be trapped in the predicament of having no resources, support, or community. Still her point was well taken, and even though we never agreed on the "right" way to understand stories about one's home, the emotional intensity of her argument was unforgettable—so powerful that our conversations linger with me to this day.

In her autobiographical writings, Angelika Bammer echoes my friend's concerns by lamenting her embarrassment to speak publicly as a German after the Shoah and by revealing a strong desire to disassociate from a cultural heritage that was embroiled in a history of violence.[23] Instead of satiating her desire to deny her heritage, Bammer continues to work through it in an effort to accept the responsibility of bearing a specific story and having a specific home. One wonders why Americans do not take this attitude of responsibility toward slavery and, moreover, if they take it on with the Iraq War. Whenever the idea of communal responsibility is broached with my students in undergraduate courses, many resist or, arguably worse, fail to fathom its relevance. They do not grasp how being part of the "American story" implicates them in the legacy of slavery, granting them an inheritance built on the oppression and exploitation of one group over and against others. Sometimes we refuse to acknowledge how we are connected to the other, we deny the metaphorical "rib" within our lives, the stories that move and mix among one another, because if we acknowledge them, we are then compelled to deal with the needs, feelings, memories, and stories of the other in our midst—all of which is an emotionally complicated process.

Bammer's struggle with her story is an important lesson for anyone who might want to ignore the call of their story. As feminists and others committed to liberation movements have long argued, identity is never neutral, and the stories that engender our hybrid identities wield widely varying amounts of power and privilege. Christians striving to emulate Jesus' other-oriented style and seriously consider the incarnation as a template for navigating hybrid existence cannot avoid dealing with power and privilege and must accept the burden of being implicated in complex and enmeshed stories—to acknowledge, respect, and manage the borders of them. The same demand goes for those who glamorize and idealize stories, notwithstanding myself, who are nostalgic about what they perceive to be their core cultural narratives. Being about borders here means upholding the borders of one's own story—for better or worse—by telling it, facing whether one's attachment to the story is related to feeling charitable or entitled, and potentially relinquishing any story that harms that of another and mourning it. Through waiting for the other in conflict, exposure, and mourning, Christians are asking the other at the border to forgive them for their trespasses. This, if only implicitly, is evident in Bammer's story. She holds on to the German

[23] Angelika Bammer, "The Dilemma of the 'But': Writing Germanness After the Holocaust," in *Borders, Exiles, Diasporas*, ed. Elazar Barkan and Marie-Denise Shelton (Stanford, CA: Stanford University Press, 1998), 15–31.

story not in arrogance or nostalgia but almost in a practice of penance. The new mortifications of Christian life are not private flagellations; instead they are public events where we embrace our stories—those good, those bad, and those overlapping and intertwining with others.

Emotional Homelessness

As each one of us accepts the responsibility of being vigilant about borders in the midst of hybrid existence, we must take great care not to fall into any hollow celebration of or casual nod to difference; instead we must maintain a posture that honors the many stories that inform our lives and connect us to that of another. We are chosen to give up feeling too comfortable with our most cherished stories. In many ways, like Jesus who is reoriented and undone by the stories of others and calls his disciples to a similar sort of existence, Christians must accept a certain type of homelessness, namely, an emotional one. Since all of our stories are connected to that of another, we forfeit exclusive claims to any one story and to any one place. When read this way, homelessness cannot be used as a rationale to be irresponsible to where one stands; rather, it demands taking seriously one's place in relation to another. In the conversation with my friend it seemed as if she and possibly others of her generation wished to sidestep being labeled German in order to escape the sins of the past. Accepting hybrid existence means that we cannot hide from any one story, as we carry the complexity of other peoples' stories in our own corporeal lives. I am proposing here that not just some of us are hybrids but rather that all of us share stories that overlap and intertwine, and hence we are called to recognize our hybrid existence. In acknowledging and embracing hybrid existence, humanity moves from a posture of feeling entitled at the borders of self, story, and place to being charitable at them.

When discussing our background with others, it helps to listen to how their stories might be different from ours and to prepare for the conflict that difference in perspective brings, the intellectual, moral, and affective dissonance that surfaces in such an honest conversation.[24] Perhaps this

[24] Michelle J. Bartel, a Presbyterian theologian, explains that while conflict can be creative and affirm one's individuality, it can be dangerous if entered into without love; see Bartel, *What It Means to Be Human: Living with Others before God* (Louisville, KY: Geneva Press, 2001). She names a fear that many of us share, that if we give in to our desire for conflict, or what she terms "strong feeling," we run the risk of spiraling

conflict could be productive and transformative, even a point of departure for conversing with them more deeply. Shifting the emotional dissonance to the foreground of a relationship exposes the limits of our knowledge about how others will react, thus undermining our safety. This is the burden and risk of hybrid existence. We must expose ourselves to being honest about the privilege associated with this or that story and be prepared to let it go in order to create space for others' to be heard and acknowledged. I would be naïve to argue that making room for another will bring instant happiness. On the contrary, relinquishing one's stories for that of another may bring anger or sadness. A period of grieving may be necessary to mourn such stories. Mourning emphasizes the reality of borders in a world in which they seem to be disappearing for any number of social reasons. Although it is a dangerous and exhausting process, being about borders may be the only option for Christians who want to seriously consider the emotional drama with others that already is unfolding in their interpersonal relations.

Summary

Every day in a variety of interpersonal contexts each one of us is transgressed by another's needs, feelings, memories, or stories, creating a situation that exposes the intimacy of borders between self and other and signals a need for charity in our most personal of relationships. The rigors of dealing with the limits of self and the demands of the other in the midst of hybrid existence was explored here in a number of settings, in terms of our body processes, family relationships, and cultural backgrounds. Maternity functioned as a metaphor for highlighting the challenges of incarnating hybrid existence—the multiple stories and overwhelming feelings that emerge when dealing with difference. I employed the motherhood model not in any nostalgic retreat about what mothers should be, but rather in an attempt to find a fresh way of thinking about the positive and negative emotional effects of living with otherness on a day-to-day basis, specifically how boundaries between self and otherness complicate our lives in ways we may never have imagined. As a symbol for being human in today's global world, mater-

---

into alienation (41). Her point is well taken, namely, that conflict should be entered into with a sense of love and charity. Still I want to push her argument further, that by entering into conflict we are already performing charity.

nity allows for the intensity of feeling that each one of us faces in the midst of others, whether the borders manifest in our embodied inter-actions with one another, between parents and children, or even on the communal level. In the following chapter, I trace how emotions unfold at the borders between Judaism and Catholicism and discuss how being vigilant about affect has the potential to influence the reception of ecclesial teachings or, at the very least, redirect religious stories in the future.

Chapter 4

The Danger of Trespass in Jewish-Catholic Relations[1]

Catholics holding seders, Jews decorating Christmas trees, their children being baptized and circumcised—with all this moving and mixing with one another how do we know who we are anymore? As porous as they are, borders among these religions do exist. We know this because we sense them. Even the most pious of believers cannot help feeling vulnerable when faced with someone who is different from them by culture, creed, and country. Being about borders in an interreligious context, consequently, demands attentiveness to the unnerving feelings that surface when one is projected from their comfort zone into the emotional chaos of hybrid existence. In what follows, I focus on the affective implications of the hybridized relations between Jewish and Catholic communities.[2] By analyzing a handful of church-related documents and

---

[1] I realize that the labels "Jewish-Christian" and "Jewish-Catholic" are contested terms, specifically that some Jews and Christians find these descriptive phrases unhelpful and even hurtful in that they ignore the complex alterity of one or the other religion. Nonetheless, I continue to use them throughout this chapter and book, not in any attempt to salvage them, rather to bring to the forefront the conflict that always is involved in any type of interreligious encounter or dialogue.

[2] As my aim is to provide everyday examples in which Christians in particular have neglected to deal with the emotional impact of otherness, for the majority of this book I generally do not distinguish among how various Jewish denominations or movements, such as Orthodox or Conservative Jewish communities, might feel differently about specific boundary situations. Nonetheless, for being about borders to

problematizing the issue of trespass in the canonization of Edith Stein, I contend that in being about borders Catholics are elected to respect the feelings of the other to the point of surrendering and mourning any entitled attachment to their own religious story.

Living in an Interreligious Family

Caring for and just plain getting along with those you love as discussed in the previous chapter is a tall order, and relating to one's siblings is no different. In the best of times they can provide camaraderie and support, while in the worst of times extreme emotions can sever the bonds between brothers and sisters, setting the scene for competition over parental affection, authority, and inheritance. It is not unusual for arguments to erupt about the past, as each family member has a unique experience of what "really" happened. After Vatican II (1962–65), the challenge of living with one's Jewish brothers and sisters became a paramount concern for Catholics, particulary with acceptance of *Nostra Aetate* (The Declaration on the Relation of the Church to Non-Christian Religions; 1965).[3]

Most broadly, *Nostra Aetate* emphasizes the connections and commonalities among the world's religions—how even the Eastern traditions of Hinduism and Buddhism share values with monotheistic religions, including a desire to understand "the unsolved riddles of human existence."[4] The declaration also concentrates on the common stories and prophets within the Abrahamic traditions of Judaism, Christianity, and Islam, ultimately cherishing the "common spiritual heritage" between Jews and Christians, a spiritual patrimony, which lends itself to "mutual understanding and appreciation."[5]

At the same time as *Nostra Aetate* illuminates the interconnections among the world's religions, it designates a clear difference between Christianity and all the "others": "The Catholic Church rejects nothing

---

emerge as a way of being human for those beyond the Christian worldview, delving into intrareligious stories and controversies most certainly would be necessary.

[3] Declaration on the Relation of the Church to Non-Christian Religions, *Nostra Aetate* (NA), 28 October 1965 in *Vatican Council II: Constitutions, Decrees, Declarations,* ed. Austin Flannery, rev. ed. (Northport, NY: Costello Publishing Co., 1996), 569–74.

[4] Ibid., par. 1.

[5] Ibid., par. 4.

of what is true and holy in these religions. It has a high regard for the manner of life and conduct, the precepts and doctrines which, although differing in many ways from its own teaching, nevertheless often reflect a ray of that truth which enlightens all men and women. Yet it proclaims and is in duty bound to proclaim without fail, Christ who is the way, the truth and the life [Jn 14:6]. In him, in whom God reconciled all things to himself (see 2 Cor 5:18-19), people find the fullness of their religious life."[6] In these few phrases, *Nostra Aetate* erects a border between Christianity and all other religions, implicitly affirming that while there may be moving and mixing among them, there is one pure and true story that leads to salvation.

Maneuvering the porous and enmeshed borders among Christianity and other religions is a formidable undertaking. In relation to Judaism, despite the fact that the declaration calls for Catholics to renounce "displays of anti-semitism," it fails to provide instructions for dealing with the affective impact of religious difference, the negative ways in which Jews and Christians may at times feel toward one another.[7] Without specific strategies for overcoming visceral reactions toward one another, how are Christians to enact the "christian charity" that this document esteems?[8] Like in the realm of one's interpersonal relations, practices that hone one's capacity for conflict, exposure, and mourning might prove useful as Catholics begin to imagine living with their Jewish siblings within this unchartered emotional terrain.

One way to conceive of the possibility of conflict, exposure, and mourning at the porous borders between Jewish and Christian communities is by returning to a theme from the previous chapter, namely that of "family." Similar border disputes crop up in the ongoing relations between Jews and Christians as do with the ones we love. *Nostra Aetate* implicitly calls Catholics to celebrate their interreligious family, highlighting their shared ancestry with those of the Jewish faith: "[T]his sacred council remembers the spiritual ties which link the people of the new covenant to stock of Abraham."[9]

[6] Ibid., par. 2.
[7] Ibid., par. 4.
[8] Ibid.
[9] Ibid.

Memory and Identity

Memory becomes an important lens for understanding the enmeshed familial relations between Christian and Jewish communities. When grappling with memory from a position of being about borders one must appreciate that remembering is always an emotionally charged process, and hence is never neutral. Various theologians grapple with the matrix of issues of memory, identity, and justice. For example, in *The End of Memory: Remembering Rightly in a Violent World*, Miroslav Volf asserts that human beings "have a *moral obligation* to remember truthfully."[10] For Volf this does not mean that remembering is free from the constraints of subjectivity, rather that when remembering one is responsible to learn about their perspective in an effort to enact justice: "The obligation to remember truthfully, and therefore to seek the truth, counters the dangers involved in claims to possess the truth. Seekers of truth, as distinct from alleged possessors of truth, will employ 'double vision'—they will give others the benefit of the doubt, they will inhabit imaginatively the world of others, and they will endeavor to view events in question from the perspective of others, not just their own."[11] Being a seeker of truth takes courage and work, and in family systems this already intricate and obligatory process is complicated further by the order in which one is born.

Most of the time, each child remembers their parents uniquely, depending on how, when, or why they were conceived and born, resulting in disparate stories about their parents' identities, hopes, dreams, and depth of affection for each of them. For example, the oldest child in a family can often pinpoint when the new child emerged onto the scene and may even be able to articulate the changes that ensued. Living as an only child, even for a brief period, the oldest in a family retains memories to which they alone are privy. Conversely, those born last are hard-pressed to recall a time when they cannot remember their sisters or brothers being present. Even if their older siblings are away at school or married, the youngest child's mental and emotional landscape is colored by consistent references to their lives. In other words, since the youngest was born, they have been dealing with the emotional impact of having siblings, possibly making the presumption that the children before them

---

[10] Miroslav Volf, *The End of Memory: Remembering Rightly in a Violent World* (Grand Rapids, MI: Eerdmans Publishing Company, 2006), 51.

[11] Ibid., 57.

perceive family life in the same way. These differing perspectives within one's family turn out to be critical when attempting to build positive relations with one another.

Catholics have much to learn from the effects of birth order and sibling relationships on one's experience and perspective. In an effort to fulfill a moral obligation to remember, they might begin to conceptualize themselves as the younger sibling, capitulating to the fact that there are some memories that are not of great consequence to them or that are even on their radar, but that profoundly influence their older sibling's sense of self, story, and place. The emotions that are connected with specific memories also need to be engaged for any type of being about borders to take shape. Given that *Nostra Aetate* does not account for these familial, psychological dynamics on one's relationships with others, it is up to Catholic individuals and communities to learn how to handle the emotional conflict that will in all probability materialize between religions. Most importantly they are compelled by the gospels to learn how to surrender and mourn any narcissistic attachment to their own stories in an attempt to honor those of their Jewish brothers and sisters.

Mourning here is both literal and metaphorical. Literally being chosen by another to yield any sense of self-righteousness about what did or did not happen means that one has to relinquish all the feelings of entitlement that go along with the so-called "one true story." This takes time and a period of concrete grieving—of reflection on how that loss shapes their present and future realities. Mourning could also be read metaphorically in that no one actually dies; rather, the idealized sense of self passes on, allowing for the ambiguity and hybridity of personal and communal stories to unfold. When a person mourns, one not only grieves the flattering and palatable side of the individual but also is confronted with the legacy of the whole person, both the good and the bad. Experiencing the positive and negative aspects of one's most intimate relationships within family settings is an important aspect of our ordinary lives, and thus when a family member passes away it practically seems like a disservice to remember merely what felt good since that is only part of the story. Being about borders means owning up to the total emotional complexity of being human, including the multifaceted dimensions of individuals and communities, the limits of human memory, and the interconnectedness of personal and communal stories. This is the implicit emotional work that occurs when Jesus' other-oriented self reaches out to those ostracized in his own community and calls his disciples then and now to do the same.

The spiritual patrimony, or the shared stories and contested memories between Jews and Catholics, is not the only reference to memory and remembering in *Nostra Aetate*. Regarding the church's encounter with Muslims, the declaration additionally calls for forgetting what impedes positive future interreligious encounter: "Over the centuries many quarrels and dissensions have arisen between Christians and Muslims. The sacred council now pleads with all to forget the past, and urges that a sincere effort be made to achieve mutual understanding; for the benefit of all, let them together preserve and promote peace, liberty, social justice and moral values."[12] Again, from a psychological perspective this is easier said than done. Getting over a painful event can be a grueling process, especially when traumatic memories transform one's identity altogether. For instance, if one lies to their sibling about an isolated event, the person duped would in all probability be able to recover from the act of deception and forgive them fairly quickly. Nonetheless, if one has experienced a pattern of being deceived since they were born, then their capacity to forgive may be curtailed by fundamental changes in their affective and cognitive processes, possibly leading them to have lifelong struggles with trust and even thwarting their ability to accept the most heartfelt of apologies. Rather than an outright forgetting, an enhanced sense of re-membering is necessary, one that lets go of and mourns the oppressive and offensive stories that caused one another's hurt feelings in the first place and one that allows for possible impasses relative to memory due to a history of injury and trauma. Only when this sort of disciplined emotional work is done can trust perhaps begin to develop between the parties in question. Generally absent from ecclesial documents, these are the intangible yet indispensable affective ingredients for a theological anthropology of difference to flourish.

In 1990, John Paul II in his address on the twenty-fifth anniversary of *Nostra Aetate* revisited the issue of memory regarding Jewish-Christian relations: "No dialogue between Christians and Jews can overlook the painful and terrible experience of the Shoah."[13] Stressing the importance of remembering the suffering of the other before enacting any initiative to connect with that person or community, this anniversary statement

[12] NA, par. 3.

[13] John Paul II, Address of His Holiness John Paul II for the 25th Anniversary Celebration of the Declaration *"Nostra Aetate,"* December 6, 1990, http://www.vatican.va/holy_father/john_paul_ii/speeches/1990/december/documents/hf_jp-ii_spe_19901206_xxv-nostra-aetate_en.html (accessed September 5, 2007), par. 4.

foreshadows later efforts to reach out to Jewish individuals and groups, including the ecclesial document, *We Remember: A Reflection on the Shoah* (1998).[14] As proactive as they may be in reaching out to the other, it is arguable that such statements do not go far enough in regaining the trust of those victimized because they do not accept more of the responsibility for being the victimizer. Merely recalling an unjust incident from the past is not what is demanded in being about borders. Again, a type of re-membering that reconfigures past events in relation with one and another's feelings is essential for charity as emotional openness to emerge and justice to prevail in a broader communal context. Volf implicitly argues for this comprehensive sense of re-membering when he claims that it "cannot refer just to what is right for that wronged person as an individual. It must mean also what is right for those who have wronged the individual and for the larger community."[15] Only when interreligious encounter is framed in more nuanced interpretations of memory and trust and when interreligious dialogue transcends mere niceties and what is considered palatable can "[c]hanges in affections, judgments, and decisions about oneself and others" take place, creating what Brad Hinze describes as a setting for "conversion, repentance, and reform."[16]

To be sure, complicating the work of memory and laying the foundation for reform cannot be accounted for by rational means only. Hinze takes one path in explaining this in his work toward a dialogical ecclesiology, where he privileges the genre of lamentation as a way of opening up to the desires and voices that are sometimes "denied or ignored" in encounter initiatives.[17] For Hinze, being attentive to expressions of anger, hurt, resentment, confusion, and so on is not a simple procedure: "To respect and seek to understand the intentions expressed by lamentations, and the deeper fears and suspicions they represent, is not to stop at intentions. Rather it is to acknowledge that there are complex and often unconscious dimensions working at the borders of intentionality. In the

---

[14] Commission for Religious Relations with the Jews, We Remember: A Reflection on the Shoah, March 16, 1998, http://www.vatican.va/roman_curia/pontifical_councils /chrstuni/documents/rc_pc_chrstuni_doc_16031998_shoah_en.html (accessed September 5, 2007).

[15] Volf, *The End of Memory*, 11.

[16] Bradford E. Hinze, "When Dialogue Leads to the Reform of Tradition," in *Tradition and Tradition Theories: An International Discussion*, ed. Thorsten Larbig and Siegfried Wiedenhofer (Münster: Lit Verlag, 2006), 337.

[17] Bradford E. Hinze, *Practices of Dialogue in the Roman Catholic Church: Aims and Obstacles, Lessons and Laments* (New York: Continuum, 2006), 245.

regions of consciousness between twilight and pitch darkness lurk deeper desires and dynamics. . . . Here too God is at work."[18]

If one takes seriously the claim that God is at work in one's affective interactions with others, then one is pressed to consider how to interpret the meaning behind the visceral reactions and expressions that surface in all types of encounter. One way according to Hinze is through "active listening" or "listening well," which "begins by conveying hospitality to another individual or group, welcoming and encouraging others to speak," to tell their stories and share their memories all the while one is being vigilant about "eye contact" and "posture" and, I would add, being watchful for bodily signs from either party of feeling just plain uncomfortable.[19]

Clinical approaches to trauma and memory can enhance Volf's and Hinze's theological initiatives for fulfilling one's obligation to re-member and for creating a context for reform by fostering situations in which individuals and communities feel safe enough with one another so that conflict, exposure, and eventually mourning can unfold. Neurologists claim that much of our understanding of self is set in a matrix of stories grounded in "memories learned through personal experience, including both conscious or explicit memories and unconscious or implicit memories."[20] As a result, memory incarnates these other dimensions of self; those "tiny spaces, the connections, between neurons" or what are commonly called the synapses are where one another's sense of self and other emerge.[21] One cannot speak of person or story without dealing with embodied experience, the very point being articulated here from a theological perspective. Deny others the possibility that their embodied experience is unique from your own and you deny the possibility of having an authentic and life-giving relationship with them.

---

[18] Ibid.

[19] Ibid., 253.

[20] Joseph LeDoux, "The Self: Clues from the Brain," *Annals of New York Academy of Sciences* 1001 (2003): 295.

[21] Ibid., 298. Anticipating that this neural reading of the self might be misunderstood as limiting, Joseph LeDoux argues that this "assertion that synapses are the basis of your personality does not assume that your personality is determined by synapses; rather, it's the other way around. Synapses are simply the brain's way of receiving, storing, and retrieving our personalities, as determined by all the psychological, cultural, and other factors, including the genetic ones" (302).

Being about borders demands a realization, even a sort of conversion to the position that the ways that human beings relate to one another are not based on a purely rational process; more than that there is an embodied basis of self that is grounded in our stories, driven by our synapses, and influenced by affect.[22] People have asymmetrical emotional responses to this or that event, creating affective disparities, which in all likelihood shape their perception of their stories and memories. When one takes seriously the emotional life of another, one needs to be prepared for the other's memories to contest their own. Moreover, as memories provide the foundation of many of our most cherished stories, when heeding another's memories it becomes imperative that we begin to open up, as difficult as it may seem, to the possibility of relinquishing our story in order to honor that of another. Being about borders demands that Christians realize the complexity of what it means to be human: that we are composed of a plurality of stories, memories, and feelings that influence our interactions with one another, and thus these all need to be re-membered, that is, put back together again, charitably at the border with another in order for life-giving relationships to flourish. Put another way, we are always developing in the presence of others, and Christians have a unique calling to be honest about the gravity of this hybridized engagement so they can relate to others at the border with a creative openness to risk and relationship rather than with resentment and hostility.

The Pain and Difficulty of Separation

Up until this point I have framed the relationship between Jews and Christians as one of siblings. In *Constantine's Sword*, James Carroll puts forth the idea that the psychic conflict between the two is more analogous to the bond between conjoined twins.[23] Thinking through this metaphor might prove helpful to our understanding of the precariousness of border life. As surgeons go to great lengths to separate the twins with precision,

---

[22] For more on the link between memory and emotion, see Antonio Damasio, *The Feeling of What Happens: Body and Emotion in the Making of Consciousness* (New York: Harcourt Brace & Company, 1999), 294. Damasio cites James McGaugh as a pioneer connecting learning with emotion, see McGaugh, *Learning and Memory: An Introduction* (San Francisco: Albion Pub. Co., 1973).

[23] James Carroll, *Constantine's Sword: The Church and the Jews* (New York: Houghton Mifflin Company, 2001), 392.

issues related to borders come to the fore. Can both babies survive the separation? Which baby is in more danger? Which is more viable? Is one organ, body part, or baby more expendable? In other words, which child has more to give or more to lose? An interesting comparison emerges when one approaches the intimate corporeal bonds between Jews and Christians like one would conjoined twins. How does one separate Jewish and Christian stories, while simultaneously supporting the other's survival? Is one part of the story more expendable than another? Which of the parties has more to give or more to lose? Catholics might consider the grave emotional implications of their intimate proximity with and radical otherness from their Jewish siblings—in other words, be vigilant about the porosity of their borders and the ambiguity their leakiness creates.

To be created in a world of diversity, to be created as hybrids, and to be chosen to imitate a "hybridized" Christ means to be comfortable with difference, not to stigmatize, erase, or avoid it, but to deal with it. As already mentioned, throughout his life Jesus shows compassion for those stigmatized in society. The gospels illustrate his posture as being open to others rather than closed off. Moreover, the incarnation reveals that difference can coexist, maybe not easily, but respectfully. Finally, while entitlement connotes a hoarding of resources, power, and place, the cross is representative of a type of kenotic existence in which all claims for pure or singular "storied" notions of self are relinquished for another. Catholics can imitate this exposure in their everyday relations with those from different faith traditions by revealing their stories and memories as similar and distinctive, by admitting that their particular beliefs may cause emotional turmoil, and by finally letting go of their lingering feelings of entitlement. Only through feeling for the other, as painful as it may be, can Christians begin to engage Jewish individuals and communities with a life-affirming openness.

The discourse of family certainly drives home the importance of addressing the emotional component of Jewish-Catholic border negotiations. It is not too strong to suggest that the numbing effects of narcissism have predisposed Christians toward typing their Jewish siblings in a role akin to the Cinderella sister, the one alienated from power and prestige and hence disposable. As long as Catholics fall short of developing empathy for Jewish individuals and communities, the spirit of *Nostra Aetate*, including its call for Catholics to remember and celebrate their shared ancestry with their Jewish siblings, cannot be cultivated. At the same time, as helpful as it is for accentuating the affective volatility of border life, employing the discourse of family when referring to the interactions between Jews and Christians is limited, in that some in the Jewish community might not recognize themselves as part of any inter-religious family and might regard this entire conversation as presumptuous.

Employing the family metaphor for conceptualizing porous borders and hybrid identity between Jews and Christians is an easy move, particularly as it is writ onto post–Vatican II conversations about interreligious dialogue. However, as my colleague, Jewish feminist theologian Judith Plaskow, has rightly pointed out, for Jewish individuals and communities, using the metaphor of family and the notion of siblings to describe the history of Jews and Christians does not necessarily make sense. A more fitting image for capturing a Jewish perspective on the relationship between Jews and Christians might be a different sort of domestic situation, according to Plaskow, one of a house in which everyone lived for a while, until the Christians moved away. While the Christians felt nostalgia for their former home, the Jewish residents updated the house and made it their own, consequently projecting these religious communities onto two very different trajectories. Plaskow's insights and this metaphor of the house become even more poignant when read onto the debate about the canonization of Edith Stein.

Such reminders about how metaphors work for some and not others are really important in keeping all of us honest about who our audience is and what our goals are, bringing us back to the importance of being about borders. *Nostra Aetate* was written for Catholics at a particular moment in history, and, as such, it cannot account for the stories or feelings of any other individual or group. What it does offer is an invitation for Catholics to reflect on porous boundaries between the Jewish and Christian traditions as well as an opportunity to realize how those leaky borders have led to enmeshed stories and contested memories—a hybridized existence—much like that found in any number of families throughout the world.

Theological Attempts at the Border

While *Nostra Aetate* highlights the overlapping and intertwining borders between Jews and Christians, there have been other ecclesial documents that have attempted to deal more directly with the ambiguity resulting from porous borders. In what follows, I review two relatively recent theological attempts at navigating the leaky boundaries between

Judaism and Christianity, *Dominus Iesus* and Reflections on Covenant and Mission, evaluating how each of these approaches handles the emotional dissonance of the moving and mixing of border life.[24]

Headed by then-Cardinal Joseph Ratzinger, now Pope Benedict XVI, in 2000 the Congregation for the Doctrine of the Faith through the declaration *Dominus Iesus* (On the Unicity and Salvific Universality of Jesus Christ and the Church) addressed the contemporary challenge of religious relativism in light of Christianity's ever-increasing encounters and dialogical initiatives with other religions. In short, the declaration interprets religious relativism as an obstacle to what some consider *the* gospel truth, specifically claiming that the "universal mission" of the church is to evangelize the nations in the name of Christ.[25] In order to fix "this relativistic mentality, which is becoming ever more common," *Dominus Iesus* states, "it is necessary above all to reassert the definitive and complete character of the revelation of Jesus Christ."[26]

One could claim that this document demonstrates a first step toward setting the stage for a type of being about borders in that it promotes the necessity of gearing up for conflict when working within interreligious contexts. *Dominus Iesus* indisputably drives home the idea that borders need to be admitted between Christianity and all other religions in order to maintain genuine relationships among one another. Moreover, it implies that avoiding conflict and denying borders is not a display of respect for the other and actually could erase the alterity of either or both parties. Nevertheless, this declaration achieves only part of the work of being about borders. By emphasizing the centrality of Christ, *Dominus Iesus* certainly leads to conflict and begs exposure; however, in the end it refuses to speak about mourning any feelings of entitlement that undermine the impact of the other at the border, thereby failing to account for the affective dissonance that emerges when one meets another with

---

[24] See The Congregation for the Doctrine of the Faith, On the Unicity and Salvific Universality of Jesus Christ and the Church (*Dominus Iesus*), August 6, 2000, http://www.vatican.va/roman_curia/congregations/cfaith/documents/rc_con_cfaith_doc_20000806_dominus-iesus_en.html (accessed September 5, 2007); and see also, The National Council of Synagogues and The Bishops' Committee for Ecumenical and Interreligious Affairs, USCCB, Reflections on Covenant and Mission, August 12, 2002, http://www.bc.edu/research/cjl/meta-elements/texts/cjrelations/resources/documents/interreligious/ncs_usccb120802.htm (accessed September 5, 2007).

[25] *Dominus Iesus*, par. 1.

[26] Ibid., par. 5.

overlapping and intertwining stories—those moments of emotional trespass that cannot easily be accounted for by mere words.

When *Dominus Iesus* does indeed reference any sort of feeling, it is in relation to the hurt experienced by the Christian community as a result of not having a unified response or consensus on any one core belief: "The lack of unity among Christians is certainly a wound for the Church."[27] Significantly, the injury considered is related to self, rather than in relation to the other. While this declaration is unwavering in its vigilance about borders in that it urges Christians to affirm their "one true story" and the centrality of Christ, it fears what I have been calling narcissistic injury in that it refuses to acknowledge the feelings of the other at the border. Put another way, it denies the porous borders and unnerving and ambiguous emotional disturbances that accompany hybrid existence.

As part of a series of conversations that Catholic and Jewish leaders have been holding for more than twenty years, in 2002 the U.S. Bishops' Committee on Ecumenical and Interreligious Affairs (BCEIA) and the National Council of Synagogues (NCS) met, the upshot of which was the collaboration on a document titled Reflections on Covenant and Mission. While *Dominus Iesus* disregards all feelings for the connectedness with others, in Reflections on Covenant and Mission, Catholic leaders present an alternative theological approach to the emotional impasse of the shared border with their Jewish siblings, one that privileges their "unique relationship," that is, a spiritual patrimony above all else.[28]

Arguably the most controversial piece of this statement refers to the Christian impulse for evangelization, which, according to the Catholic contributors to the document, cannot be performed as a simple act of conversion, that is to say, "the seeking of new candidates for baptism."[29] Echoing previous comments made by John Paul II in the encyclical, On the Permanent Validity of the Church's Missionary Mandate (*Redemptoris Missio*; 1990), Reflections on Covenant and Mission insists that new and more complex forms of evangelization manifest in a myriad of settings, including "the Church's activities of presence and witness; commitment to social development and human liberation; Christian worship, prayer, and contemplation; interreligious dialogue; and proclamation and catechesis," in other words, in practices that do not overtly strive to convert others by "absorb[ing] the Jewish faith into Christianity and so end the

---

[27] Ibid., par. 17.
[28] Reflections on Covenant and Mission.
[29] Ibid.

distinctive witness of Jews to God in human history."[30] Within this document there is an untiring vigilance to the distinct story and identity of the Jewish community, in which any narrow definition of evangelization distorts, ignores, or erases: "[The church] now recognizes that Jews are also called by God to prepare the world for God's kingdom. Their witness to the kingdom, which did not originate with the Church's experience of Christ crucified and raised, must not be curtailed by seeking the conversion of the Jewish people to Christianity."[31] Their particular story results in Christians not having to feel obligated to convert them in the provincial sense of the word. Implicitly, any and all feeling engaged by this document is directed toward heeding the needs of the other at the border, rather than protecting and policing one's communal boundaries.

Reflections on Covenant and Mission seeks to accomplish precisely what *Dominus Iesus* fails to do: to be vigilant about the physical and emotional suffering caused by Christianity's entitled stance at the borders, that is, by "the history of Christians forcibly baptizing Jews."[32] Reflections on Covenant and Mission attempts to work through this legacy of trauma by opening to the emotional liminality of border life, paying attention to the other's stories, memories, and feelings to the point of giving up what some consider a central axiom of Christian identity, evangelization in the form of conversion.

Still, it is open to debate whether Reflections on Covenant and Mission misses the mark in gearing up for conflict and opening to exposure, both of which are significant aspects of an anthropology based on affectivity. To be about borders, Catholics must ask if denying an aspect of their identity by refusing a certain type of proselytizing risks obscuring the particularity of one another, including both what it means to be Jewish and what it means to be Christian. Cardinal Avery Dulles's widely publicized reaction to the statement conveys this precise danger:

> It has been well said that those who withdraw from evangelization weaken their own faith. Once we grant that there are some persons for whom it is not important to acknowledge Christ, to be baptized and to receive the sacraments, we raise questions about our own

---

[30] Ibid. See John Paul II, On the Permanent Validity of the Church's Missionary Mandate (*Redemptoris Missio*), December 7, 1990, http://www.vatican.va/holy_father/john_paul_ii/encyclicals/documents/hf_jp-ii_enc_07121990_redemptoris-missio_en.html (accessed September 5, 2007).

[31] Reflections on Covenant and Mission.

[32] Ibid.

religious life. If we are convinced that baptism incorporates us into the body of Christ and that the Eucharist nourishes us with his flesh and blood, we will be eager to share these gifts as widely as possible. Our Jewish brothers and sisters could question our sincerity if we were to tell them that the blessings of the New Covenant need not concern them. The document *Covenant and Mission* does not forthrightly present what I take to be the Christian position on the meaning of Christ for Judaism.[33]

This response recently was followed by A Note on Ambiguities Contained in Reflections on Covenant and Mission from the Committee on Doctrine and Committee on Ecumenical and Interreligious Affairs of the United States Conference of Catholic Bishops in 2009.[34] This statement attempts to clarify that the original document was not an official position from the bishops, rather part of a dialogue of leaders. Among other points, the Note also states that by not affirming that "the Church's belief that Jesus Christ in himself fulfills God's revelation begun with Abraham and that proclaiming this good news to all the world is at the heart of her mission" in many ways "presents a diminished notion of evangelization."[35] This perspective, while a step back for many committed to Jewish-Christian dialogue since Vatican II, is evidence that being in relationship with the other cannot be solved by documents alone. There are deep emotional ties to beliefs that need to be acknowledged before any one statement can fix the years of hurt and distrust between differing individuals and communities. Perhaps for Dulles, and possibly for supporters of the Note, being about borders, exposing oneself and one's stories to one another, even if that revelation causes discomfort, is the only viable option.

As we revisit these statements on Jewish-Catholic encounter, which began to emerge almost a half of a century ago, it is worth noting that only very recently have scholars begun to explore the emotional impact of encounter and the need for nontheological approaches to the issue of

---

[33] Avery Dulles, "Covenant and Mission," *America: The National Catholic Weekly* 187, no. 12 (October 21, 2002): http://www.americamagazine.org/content/article.cfm?article_id=2550 (accessed September 5, 2007).

[34] Committee on Doctrine and Committee on Ecumenical and Interreligious Affairs, USCCB, "A Note on Ambiguities Contained in 'Reflections on Covenant and Mission,'" June 18, 2009, http://www.ccjr.us/dialogika-resources/documents-and-statements/roman-catholic/us-conference-of-catholic-bishops/578-usccb-09june18 (accessed June 30, 2010).

[35] Ibid., par. 6.

engaging difference. Such explorations need to continue and sharpen in their focus as theological approaches to the border will continue to fall short and even fail, if those approaches are solely based on reason or what is often considered in the West as "rational." We have seen this failure in *Dominus Iesus* as it refuses to allow the affective disturbances that accompany hybrid existence. We have seen this failure in Reflections on Covenant and Mission as it fails to assume the charitable posture of being about borders in that it avoids the emotional complexity of conflict altogether. More than words are needed, namely, attention and embrace of affect at the borders of religious worldviews.

Living at the contact zones between Christianity and Judaism is a complicated, emotionally charged process. And instead of being vigilant about emotions, many of us focus our energies on either patrolling the borders for heretics or ignoring the borders altogether with a guise of niceness. Neither of these approaches to borders is adequate or life-giving since both refuse to acknowledge the other as other with potentially overlapping stories, thus genuinely engaging hybrid existence in any honest and, more important, charitable way. I have attempted to argue here that being open to the emotional complexity of border life, rather than superficialities, is the only long-term protection against repeating the sinful trespasses of the past and for preventing negative feelings from escalating into violence in the future. If we take an incarnational approach to understanding the borders between Judaism and Christianity, then in many ways we are called to honor the mystery of the "union" between the two traditions at the same time as we are to be vigilant about the two distinct spatial trajectories of them. This interreligious family is bonded in an asymmetrical relationship in which the distinctiveness of both parties is maintained in mysterious proximity.

Border Violations—Edith Stein:
Whose Saint? Whose Story?[36]

When embroiled in conflict it is not unusual for one family member or another to try to ameliorate the explosive situation by mentioning a common event or idea on which everyone seems to agree. Even those

---

[36] For an in-depth account of Stein's life see, Waltraud Herbstrith, *Edith Stein: A Biography*, trans. Bernard Bonowitz, 2nd Eng. ed. (San Francisco: Ignatius Press, 1992). For an interesting look at Stein's life from both Jewish and Christian communities, see Waltraud Herbstrith, ed., *Never Forget: Christian and Jewish Perspectives on Edith*

efforts at keeping the peace can spiral into contentious disputes, revealing deep emotional rifts that cannot be easily covered up by window dressing, but rather need to be treated directly through conflict, exposure, and mourning. In the ongoing relations between Jews and Christians, John Paul II's beatification (1987) and then canonization (1998) of Sister Teresa (Teresia) Benedicta of the Cross, or Edith Stein, has come to signify one such ill-fated initiative for peace, creating what some might consider to be a tipping point in Jewish-Catholic relations.

The Theopolitics of Storytelling

Stein's life story is the stuff of controversy. Born on October 12, 1891, and raised in a culturally assimilated German Jewish family, Stein came to study philosophy under the tutelage of Edmund Husserl.[37] It is written that perhaps influenced by friends, pressured by the public disdain for Jews in the academy, or due to her spiritual affinity for the mystical life of Teresa of Avila, Stein converted to Roman Catholicism in her thirties and later became a Carmelite nun.[38] Even after fleeing to Holland after Christians of Jewish descent were threatened, she was unable to escape the wrath of the Nazi regime. In August of 1942, Stein was deported with her sister Rosa and murdered in Auschwitz.

To some, her life might seem like a clear case of another person dying at the hands of a madman. Nonetheless, there is a lot at stake for those committed to being about borders in telling Stein's story, starting with the nature of her conversion. Currently, there is a border dispute over the issue of whether she converted to Catholicism from Judaism or from atheism.[39] I use the language of border dispute because one's perspective

---

Stein, trans. Susanne Batzdorff (Washington, DC: ICS Publications/Institute of Carmelite Studies, 1998).

[37] Her dissertation under Husserl was on empathy as an act of cognition, see *On the Problem of Empathy: The Collected Works of Edith Stein*, vol. 3, trans. Waltraut Stein, 3rd rev. ed. (Washington, DC: ICS Publications, 1989).

[38] Her experience of being female, Jewish, and then later Catholic in a predominately male field influenced her life's work and writings to the extent that she is regarded by some as one of the most important feminist Catholic voices of the twentieth century; see *Essays on Woman: The Collected Works of Edith Stein*, vol. 2, ed. L. Gelber and Romaeus Leuven, trans. Freda Mary Oben, 2nd rev. ed. (Washington, DC: ICS Publications, 1996).

[39] For some reflections on the depth of Stein's knowledge and affiliation with Judaism, see Susanne Batzdorff, "Life in a Jewish Family: Aunt Edith's Legacy to Her

on why she converted in the first place results in both private and public visceral reactions. Some hagiographic materials regarding Stein uphold the view that she converted to Catholicism after a period of being an atheist. This standpoint avoids any triumphalist or supersessionist readings of her life, which may attempt to suggest that during her lifetime she outright rejected Judaism in favor of Catholicism. Other hagiographies frame her life as a bridge between the Jewish and Catholic traditions, maintaining that she never lost touch with her Jewish roots. While the "one true story" behind her conversion will in all probability not be resolved in the near future, the discussion of it reveals how many Catholic and Jewish individuals and communities are still dealing with the emotional fallout from their enmeshed borders.

More divisive an issue than the nature of her conversion is the topic of her death, specifically whether she died a martyr, and if so, for whom or what? In a commonsense manner, martyrdom means dying for one's beliefs and witnessing to what one considers to be the truth at all costs. Regarding Stein, the matter is more complicated: "Was Edith Stein gassed because she was a Catholic nun and thus because of her witness of faith for Christ (the traditional meaning of martyrdom)? Or did she, together with her sister Rosa and many others, suffer this fate because of her Jewish origins? If Edith Stein is considered a martyr, what about the millions of murdered Jews?"[40] It seems as if everyone has their own version of Stein, that she was a Jew, not a Jew, a nun in the crossfire, a martyr, and so on—all of which have their own emotional complications. What is clear from John Paul II's homily at her beatification is that her official cause was one of martyrdom: "Edith Stein died at the Auschwitz extermination camp, the daughter of a martyred people. . . . This is the cause of martyrdom suffered by Sister Teresa Benedicta a Cruce together with her sister, Rosa, who has also sought refuge with the Carmelites in Echt [Holland]."[41]

Descendants," in *Never Forget*, 29–47. See also Stein's autobiographical reflections on religion in, *Life in a Jewish Family: The Collected Works of Edith Stein*, vol. 1, ed. L. Gelber and Romaeus Leuven, trans. Josephine Koeppel (Washington, DC: ICS Publications, 1986).

[40] Anna Maria Strehle, "Edith Stein's Beatification: Annoyance or Sign of Reconciliation?" in *Never Forget*, 18.

[41] John Paul II, "The Pope's Homily at her Beatification," in Craig Driscoll's *Of the Cross: The Life of Blessed Edith Stein* (Manila, Philippines: Sinag-Tala Publishers, 1987), 34.

Kenneth L. Woodward argues that one of the reasons why the church chose to declare her a martyr was to "suggest that the Catholic Church, as a church, had not nurtured blood witness to the crimes and horrors of the Nazis. To the bishops of Germany and Poland, this was a distortion of history that the church had to correct."[42] Here, I am asking a slightly different question, namely if recognizing Stein as a martyr within the catastrophic backdrop of Auschwitz breaches a border? For Jewish individuals and communities the Shoah is not just an event in Jewish history but a defining moment in how many Jews understand themselves, to the extent that the lingering traumatic feelings associated with the Shoah have been used to secure certain boundaries between Jews and all others. When Catholics claim Stein as a martyr, it is not out of the realm of possibility that they trespass those boundaries. In the aftermath of her canonization, Catholics are elected to reflect on whether such trespass was done in charity or entitlement, requiring a more rigorous analysis of for whom or for what she was martyred. Eugene J. Fisher puts it best: "This is the fear that by pointing such a bright spotlight on a Christian victim of the Holocaust, the Catholic Church might be in some way trying to turn itself, in history's memory, into its chief victim, thus at once glossing over the historical culpability of so many Christians in the deed and, in effect, appropriating the Holocaust as primarily an event of Christian martyrdom."[43]

With all these theological, political, and emotional issues at stake, how is one to narrate her death? On the one hand, her death could be read to symbolize a Christlike solidarity with those suffering. Hagiographers interpret her new name as a Carmelite nun to foreshadow such a Christic sacrifice: "She received a new name for her life, Sister Benedicta of the Cross. Teresa, after her beloved St. Teresa, Benedicta for her fond memories of the Benedictine Abbey of Beuron and 'of the Cross' for the future, a future Edith already knew would hold much suffering for her."[44] In some circles, her solidarity with those suffering is read as directed toward Catholics; in other words, she was targeted by the Nazis because she was a Catholic nun, and thus her death is an example of Catholic martyrdom, rather than of Jewish persecution. When understood from this perspective, her death is usually contextualized in the events that ensued

[42] Kenneth L. Woodward, *Making Saints: How the Catholic Church Determines Who Becomes a Saint, Who Doesn't, and Why* (New York: Simon and Schuster, 1990), 139.

[43] Eugene J. Fisher, "Edith Stein and Catholic-Jewish Relations," in *Never Forget*, 168.

[44] Driscoll, *Of the Cross*, 25.

directly before her arrest, particularly when the Dutch bishops promulgated a pastoral letter denouncing the Nazi deportations. Read in many of the churches throughout the Netherlands on July 26, 1942, the letter is thought to have instigated the Nazis to retaliate by enacting a widespread campaign against Catholic Jews, a category in which Stein found herself.[45] Contrary to being thought of as a martyr for Catholics, others read her death as a sign of Christic solidarity with the millions of Jews suffering under the Nazis. Even her nephew figures her death this way: "Edith Stein's journey from Holland to Auschwitz was, in her view, a way of the cross like that of Jesus at Golgotha. This way of the cross meant being imprisoned in a cattle car under dreadful sanitary conditions. To perish in a gas chamber was Edith Stein's cross."[46]

It is noteworthy that when her death is read as being connected to Jewish individuals and communities, it is at times translated into an offer of atonement for Jewish individuals and communities who refused to believe that Jesus is the Christ. As shocking and off-putting as this may be, there are more than a few references like the following that suggest that she died for the sake of Jewish people, not necessarily in solidarity with them, but rather in an effort to bring them to Christ:

> Upon leaving [during her arrest in Echt], she [Edith] whispered to the nuns, "Please pray, sisters!" A couple of blankets and a little food were given to Edith. The Mother Prioress gave Edith and Rosa her blessing. Then in a moment the nuns watched Edith and Rosa walk calmly out to the street and into the police van. The van drove away. With tears in her eyes the Mother Prioress recalled a request Edith had made on Passion Sunday. "Please Reverend Mother, let me offer my life to the Sacred Heart of Jesus for peace, for the conversion of my people. Let me offer my life as a victim."[47]

There are even more references to her paying the price for so-called Jewish sins, including allusions to her being born on Yom Kippur, the high holy day of atonement in Judaism, in which she and others interpret as foreshadowing her suffering and sacrifice on behalf of Jewish nonbelievers.[48]

---

[45] For more details on the religious and political events surrounding Stein's murder, see Joachim Köhler, "Companion in Human Fate," in *Never Forget*, 152–55.

[46] Gerhard Stein, "My Experiences with My Aunt Edith," in *Never Forget*, 57.

[47] Driscoll, *Of the Cross*, 30.

[48] In *Life in a Jewish Family*, Stein elaborates on the attraction of this holy day for her as a child, a nostalgia that may have stayed with her as an adult. See also, Stein, "My

Not surprisingly, more than a few in the Jewish community are out-raged that one's murder in Auschwitz could ever be understood as a sacrifice, and no less one for Jewish conversion. It is one thing to be in solidarity with those suffering, but it is another to envision oneself as substituting for another's sins of disbelief. When Catholics frame her as a martyr and portray her murder at Auschwitz as somehow redemptive, they chance ignoring the experience of the others' senseless murders. Sentiments like these rewrite the history of the Shoah into something potentially salvific, ignoring the traumatic story of the other: "On August 9th 1942 Edith Stein, prisoner number 44074, and her beloved Rosa entered the gas chamber at Auschwitz. Edith's sacrifice was now complete. Her mission fulfilled."[49] In being about borders, one is called to question whether this type of storytelling about her suffering and death distorts the events of the Shoah and the stories of Jewish com-munities. Does telling her story in terms of a sacrifice and asserting that her death is somehow didactic or redemptive for the Jewish community concretize the conviction that genocide of the Jewish community is some-how connected to or approved by God?

To formally venerate Stein without dealing with the emotional as well as theological and political implications of her life story is contrary to what I have been calling for in being about borders because it makes what appears to be another's story, the Shoah, a Christian one. In being about borders, one is faced with two tasks: sensing otherness and dealing with it charitably, meaning being open to the emotional needs of the other. It is not too strong to suggest that in honoring Stein and telling her story this way, Catholics publicly refuse to respect their limits. What-ever really happened in her life is impossible to be faithful to, but one thing is for certain, Catholics concerned with being about borders must decide who has the right to appropriate her story, in particular to narrate it, own it, and define its borders.

Experiences with My Aunt Edith," in *Never Forget*, 57. More directly, the connection between suffering and redemption is evident in her theological writings; see *Science of the Cross: The Collected Works of Edith Stein*, vol. 6, ed. L. Gelber and Romaeus Leuven, trans. Josephine Koeppel (Washington, DC: ICS Publications, 1998). Interestingly, Woodward explores how church leaders originally framed her cause as being mar-tyred for the unbelief of her people, that is, the Jews, raising all sorts of concerns about Catholic supersessionist and triumphalist attitudes. Nevertheless, as Woodward notes, John Paul II ultimately makes no mention of this idea in his homily at her beatification, see Woodward, *Making Saints*, 135–47.

[49] Driscoll, *Of the Cross*, 32.

Taking Another's Place at the Borders

In reading through the ever-expanding literature on Stein, it is tough not to get caught up in the religious and emotional fervor of her life. The point of this chapter is not to debate whether she should have been made a saint because she was holy or not but rather to reflect on whether the very valorization and rewriting of her story for purposes of canonization trespasses on and even usurps the story and place of another. To some, this entire conversation about rights to a person's life story may seem ridiculous. No one owns another's life; no one can control how someone feels about this or that person. After all, this is precisely what I argue in this book, that one's emotive reaction to a person or situation is often unpredictable and uncontrollable. While one cannot control another's reaction, however, one can and does have an ethical obligation to take note of the other's feelings. Regarding her canonization, if some members of the Jewish community find it unconscionable that Catholics would name Stein a saint because that somehow eclipses her Jewish origins and her and others' fate in the Shoah, then Catholics who are serious about being about borders need to pause and listen, so the situation of conflict does not escalate into one of violence.

Emmanuel Levinas, in thinking through the ethical implications of Martin Heidegger's *Dasein*, posits some interesting questions about one's relationship to another, which might help further flesh out our discussion of what is at stake in being about borders. Levinas writes: "My place in being, the *Da-* of my *Dasein* [the there of my being-there]—isn't it already usurpation, already violence with respect to the other."[50] Like the narcissist, *Dasein* has an unbounded sense of self, which allows him act as if the whole world is for his use, even encouraging his appropriation of the other's story and place for his own benefit. Suspicious of this uncritical sense of being human, Levinas goes as far as to wonder "*Do I have the right to be?*"[51]

There is a double meaning to Levinas's reading of the notion of place in being. In one sense, taking the other's place represents a way of opening to a relationship of charity, thereby rejecting an attitude of entitlement. This might involve going without food so another person could eat and, even more pertinent to this study, risking being in an affectively charged

---

[50] Emmanuel Levinas, *Alterity and Transcendence*, trans. Michael B. Smith (New York: Columbia University Press, 1999), 179.

[51] Ibid.

relationship with another. Taking the other's place alternatively could manifest as a posture of entitlement, in hoping to gain something at the cost of another, taking more than one's share, and, more important for this study, running roughshod over another's feelings, memories, and stories. In thinking through the double meaning of place, Catholics might reflect on how their use of Stein's life might overtake another's story and place at the borders and ultimately question whether the church violated borders between Judaism and Christianity when it made Stein a saint. In other words, does the church's fascination with Stein wrongly appropriate or colonize the Jewish experience of suffering in the Shoah? Furthermore, if one takes John Paul II's remarks on the twenty-fifth anniversary of *Nostra Aetate* seriously, Catholics after the Shoah have no choice other than to reimagine their identity, not in terms of being entitled to this or that or Stein's story, but rather by way of embracing the cathartic process of mourning, of relinquishing the feelings that rationalize any suffering of their Jewish brother or sister at the border.

In response to Stein's canonization, Daniel Polish, who has written widely on Jewish life and ritual, points out how the church chose not to respect the borders between Judaism and Catholicism, arguing that by regarding her as a bridge between Jews and Christians, some Catholics deny the doctrinal, historical, and emotional boundaries between the two world religions. He writes: "The paradox is that while for Hitler there was no way one could cease to be a Jew, from a Jewish perspective one can choose to leave Jewish life. . . . [W]hich understanding of Jewish identity will it [the church] choose to embrace: that of Edith Stein's murderers or that of the Jewish people themselves?"[52] In probing which story about Jewish identity Catholics are listening to, he also laments the church's refusal to hear her family's emotional pain resulting from her conversion, "the sense of abandonment and betrayal that they expressed."[53] These queries for Polish culminate in his repudiation of the categories of Jewish-Christian and Jewish-Catholic altogether, as they gloss over difference and reflect an implicit narcissistic stance on the part of Christians to manipulate Stein's Jewish past for their own means:

---

[52] Daniel F. Polish, "The Canonization of Edith Stein," in *Never Forget*, 171–72. It is noteworthy that there is a diversity of perspectives within Judaism on what makes a person Jewish. For more on this ambiguity related to Stein, see Menahem Benhayim, "Of Saints and Martyrs," in *Never Forget*, 133–34.

[53] Polish, "The Canonization of Edith Stein," 172.

Implicit in the Christian comfortableness with the locution "Jewish-Christian" seems to be the belief that one can embrace Christian faith and remain, in some way, part of the Jewish people. From the perspective of Jewish self-understanding, this is an impossibility. One cannot be a Jew and a Christian. To Jews the phrase "Jewish-Christian" is an oxymoron. . . .

The employment of the phrase "Jewish-Christian" to describe Edith Stein, especially in light of the exalted place in the Catholic Church to which she has now been elevated, suggests to some that there is a programmatic purpose to which her memory is being put.[54]

Reflecting on Polish's comments, does writing Stein's story in a way that stresses Catholic loss during the Shoah and that assumes an easy familial relation between Jews and Christians, like the one Plaskow previously problematized, take the other's place at the border? As there is no easy answer to this question, the emotional turmoil caused by her canonization is a sign that indeed some sort of border has been trespassed. Healing can only begin and justice can only emerge when Catholics are courageous enough to be open to the conflict and vulnerability that Stein's canonization creates and also to prepare for a time of mourning, of letting go of all attachments and claims to Stein's story for the sake of their relationship with those they perceive to be their older brothers and sisters. Catholics may have to admit to what they narcissistically are holding on to in their debate about the "one true story" regarding the Shoah and Edith Stein's place in it. This comes with its own challenges because both parties have deep memories and emotions enmeshed with their stories about Stein or others like her. Whatever the case, it becomes apparent that for Christians, mourning can never be merely for self but must always be outwardly directed and connected with the emotional life of others. Attempting to create a religious and psychic place to deal with any and all of these emotions, I am suggesting that borders can serve as places for all of humanity, and particularly for Christians, to mourn.

Studying her life, it seems to me that Edith Stein is evidence of the turf war that emerges in interreligious encounter, the agitation that bubbles up at holiday parties and interreligious family celebrations. Her life story presents Jewish and Christian communities with Jean François Lyotard's *differend*, "a case of conflict, between (at least) two parties, that cannot

---

[54] Ibid., 172, 173.

be equitably resolved for a lack of rule of judgment applicable to both parties."[55] This results in a standoff at the border, when words fail or when words are used in dialogue without attentiveness to the particular emotional effect they might have on one group or another. This is the hallmark of border life, when the emotive tenor amplifies as both parties emerge from such different experiences that communication breaks down because the available discourse cannot capture the emotion behind the disparate stories and memories. In other words, this is when, at least for now, there is simply nothing more to say. If one party attempts to push for a consensus at the border in order to avoid continuing the affectively charged discourse, then the other party's feelings might become more desperate and extreme. Being forced into having the same perspective, memory, or feeling as another is rarely possible, and the coercion it necessitates runs the risk of inciting even more affective dissonance and ultimately violence. This is the problem that Rabbi Polish points to—the violence that emerges when Catholics overtake Stein's story, and consequently Jewish borders, all in the name of Jewish-Catholic relations.

What is the Christian response then? If not storytelling and trying to relate to one's Jewish brother or sister through naming commonalities, what are the options? Gearing up for conflict is one alternative at the borders. Conflict as a denuding of oneself, a laying of oneself bare in the face of another is frightening. In such situations one fears how their vulnerability will be received and perceived. Will my initiatives be reciprocated? Will they lead to my demise? As already stated, many consequently avoid conflict *not* out of a sense of justice as it is often rationalized, but out of a sense of fear and a desire for self-preservation. In canonizing someone as controversial as Stein, Catholics must be prepared to welcome these protests and reservations, say how they are different from Jews, and also be ready to hear their older siblings out. Catholics attempting to imitate the other-oriented Christ are chosen to seek out the conflictual nature of their relationship with their Jewish brothers and sisters in charity, by admitting that they may have been hasty in honoring Stein, not because she is not holy enough to be a saint, but because her life story is experienced much differently by many in the Jewish community. Without a doubt, honoring Stein in this very public venue has unleashed many visceral reactions, all of which need to be embraced.

---

[55] Jean François Lyotard, *The Differend: Phrases in Dispute*, trans. Georges Van Den Abbeele (Minneapolis: University of Minnesota Press, 1988), xi.

Being prepared for conflict is not all that is needed here, one also needs to be open to exposure. To be sure, Christians need to be able not only to reveal their beliefs but also to expose their intense feelings at the border, so a more human and filial relationship can develop, and this may ultimately require being honest about their intellectual and emotional attachments to claims about the particular salvific nature of Christ. Exposure, however, does not always involve speaking and sometimes can unfold in silence. Lyotard's work becomes most helpful here as he proposes that there is that which cannot be expressed, feelings of conflict that go beyond linguistic discourse. In lieu of rational discourse, Lyotard emphasizes the human responsibility to signify this conflict and expose one's limits through bearing witness to it. Bearing witness to the *differend* involves acknowledging this affective dimension of being human, as well as attempting to find new idioms to express it. In being about borders, Catholics might do well to think of Edith Stein as a signifier of the *differend*, a reminder that sometimes there is nothing more to say.

Maybe the affective overflow surrounding the canonization of Edith Stein has showed Catholics and Jews that there are occasions when in many ways we are, in the words of Levinas, "beyond dialogue," meaning beyond the superficial sameness that commonsense conversation often demands.[56] For Levinas, being beyond dialogue requires an affective vigilance to what divides us, whether that is race, religion, story, culture, and so on. At times, the only just action is to witness to difference by standing silent at the borders, admitting the separation between self and other, and declaring the inability to speak with one another in any intelligible or constructive way. Levinas writes:

> Neither violence, nor guile, nor simple diplomacy. Nor simple tact, nor pure tolerance, nor even simple sympathy, nor even simple friendship—that attitude before insoluble problems, what can it be, and what can it contribute?
>
> What can it be? The presence of persons before a problem. Attention and vigilance: not to sleep until the end of time, perhaps. The presence of persons, who, for once, do not fade away into words, get lost in technical questions, freeze up into institutions or structures. The presence of persons in the full force of their irreplaceable identity, in the full force of their inevitable responsibility. To recognize and name those insoluble substances and keep them from

---

[56] Levinas, *Alterity and Transcendence*, 79.

exploding in violence, guile or politics, to keep watch where conflicts tend to break out, a new religiosity and solidarity—is loving one's neighbour anything other than this?[57]

Is it plausible that silence is a way of mourning the loss of the right story, of thinking that one has all the answers, and of admitting the emotional complexity of hybrid existence? Is it conceivable that the mystery of the incarnation, the inscrutability of the hypostatic union, calls Christians to a way of living with not fully knowing the other, and yet still being respectful of the other in such intense proximity? Perhaps truly loving the other is surrendering and mourning the desire to know them completely and to live with the sometimes uncomfortable situation of emotional impasse.

In the previous chapter, I argued that trespass can be a good thing, a charitable act, meaning sometimes we have to leave the security of what we perceive as our place to be in relationship with another. We have to trespass the accepted boundary as a way of demonstrating compassion and love for the one on the other side or in the spaces in-between. In Jewish-Catholic relations, however, it seems as if most acts of trespass are representative of a posture of entitlement rather than charity. Reading through some of the literature on Stein, the emotional tone of many of the articles is blatant. In being about borders, Christians and here Catholics are called to be attentive to how her canonization sets off emotions and wonder why. Even if it does not seem rational, being charitable means pausing and understanding why it is creating such a fury from the perspective of the other, in other words, acknowledging that another's story matters not just in words, but in feelings and actions. Being about borders in the midst of Jewish-Catholic relations means admitting and privileging Jewish difference and mourning silently an idealized place of one's own at the borders.

Summary

Living with others, being open to the emotionally tinged give-and-take of relationships of difference, is what I mean by being about borders. In being about borders nothing is nonnegotiable because one's every thought, action, and feeling is influenced by that of another. In relation

---

[57] Ibid., 87–88.

to Jewish-Christian encounters, embracing this type of being entails a complex emotional process in which one is called to open to the conflict that arises from contested memories and stories, to reveal the stories that are used to protect one's privilege at the expense of another, and to mourn one's attachment to self, story, and place at the border for the sake of one another. Post–Vatican II insights and events make clear that respecting the Jewish community demands more than tolerating it; instead Christians are called to negotiate their identity in relation to their Jewish brothers and sisters as they realize that Jewish identity and suffering has an impact on Christian storytelling. This is difficult emotional work, unnatural to most of us, so much so that Christians might benefit from learning about clinical research on trauma-like situations and integrating it into their everyday encounters with others. Before moving to contemporary approaches to trauma, it is necessary to investigate being about borders within the larger scale of geopolitics. So now I turn to the Israeli-Palestinian challenge of being about borders, more specifically what Christians in the United States might learn from their stories.

Chapter 5

Surrendering Place in the Global Landscape

Whether encountering others within the safe confines of one's kitchen or through the precarious venue of the internet, Christians in particular are called to attend to the emotionally volatile pulse of border life in an effort to live as Jesus did. Unlike borders in interpersonal and interreligious relations, some borders in the global landscape offer a clarity defined by the natural geography of the land. Being about borders in any context, however, requires one to question that clarity and prioritize the affective dimensions of dealing with difference by being vigilant about the stories told regarding where, when, and why borders were created in the first place. This is especially important since in many cases, "[s]o-called 'natural' boundaries are simply the superimposition of human assumptions on geographical features."[1] Through exploring specific stories told about the border disputes between the Israelis and the Palestinians, including the "human assumptions" about them, I hope to tease out some of the broader issues related to what it is at stake in being about borders in the global panorama, especially for Christians in the United States who continue to struggle with the call to be charitable to others.

In each of the previous border disputes, including the chapter on bodily matters and the chapter on interreligious encounter, I have what

[1] Bernard Wasserstein, *Israelis and Palestinians: Why Do They Fight? Can They Stop?* (New Haven, CT: Yale University Press, 2003), 99.

is often referred to as "first-hand" experience. With no such direct experience in this global conflict, it is right to question if I am overstepping my own boundaries. Whenever "others" like me approach the highly contentious issues of this region in the Middle East, it could appear that we are indulging in a voyeuristic desire to consume and exploit the other's tragedy. Conscious of this danger, in this book and particularly in this chapter, I struggle to be about borders myself. In being about borders here, my work is not an intervention for one side or the other but rather an attempt to demonstrate that wherever we live, we have an obligation to be attentive to the affective dissonance that hybrid existence brings.

As one might imagine, the border disputes between the Israelis and the Palestinians are particularly rich because of the complicated interplay between geopolitical and religious issues. Anton La Guardia in *War Without End* explains this dynamic:

> The conflict over the Holy Land—or Israel, or Palestine—is a vast story of tragedy and redemption. . . . There is a constant moral tension about the place—the survival of the ancient amidst the new, the superposition of the religious and the profane, the sullying of the spiritual with the brutal, the discordance between epic heroism and pettiness. This attempt to reconcile the earthly Jerusalem with the heavenly Jerusalem makes the country compelling and tragic.
>
> The creation of Israel, and its conflict with Palestinians, are sagas that seem to start with Abraham and are still unfolding before our eyes. It is as if we were still witnessing the sibling rivalries of the Bible. We feel outrage at Cain for the murder of Abel. We are torn between the rights of Ishmael, Abraham's first-born, and Isaac the true son born of Sarah. We witness Jacob's deception in taking Esau's birthright, and watch in wonder at the magnanimity of Joseph toward his treacherous brothers.[2]

Being about borders in this thorny setting requires being attentive to the intricate dance between religion and politics and realizing that separating these two dimensions of border life is not always feasible. Overlapping issues exacerbate "old wounds" between both parties, setting the stage in which "ancient competitions and conflicts are given a quality

---

[2] Anton La Guardia, *War Without End: Israelis, Palestinians, and the Struggle for a Promised Land* (New York: St. Martin's Press, 2001), 366–67.

of cosmic significance."[3] Unlike the other border disputes analyzed in this book, the stories about one another's pain and injury in relation to the Israeli-Palestinian context are unabashedly public, and as a result they overflow the land of the olive trees, creating food for thought for the rest of the world.

Contested Land, Contested Story

I have a lifelong friend who is an amazing storyteller. She knows exactly which events to play up, what gestures to use, and when to change voice pitch and rhythm to maintain her audience's attention. Perhaps out of petty jealousy of her uncanny ability to read the emotional pulse of the situation or because of my own rigid preoccupation with what I consider to be the truth, sometimes when she tells a story, I find myself wanting to blurt out, "That is not exactly what happened! That is not the true story!" For my friend and her audience, her version is the right one. She knows even if unconsciously that content can never be separated from performance and that while storytelling entails a sense of the truth, it is a different animal altogether as it opens gracefully to the emotional complexity of our humanity. Whenever she tells a story, she develops characters with intriguing histories and focuses on a pivotal event in order to create the desired emotional effect in her audience. Public instances of storytelling like those surrounding Israeli-Palestinian relations hinge on the same need for affectively appealing characters and life-altering events. Those interested in being about borders need to be open to and even vigilant about these emotionally charged dimensions of stories and storytelling, sometimes even more than they need to get the story straight.

Privileging de facto the emotional implications of the larger narrative over the specific facts of what happened might make some individuals nervous or just plain uncomfortable. Volf expresses this precise anxiety in his work on memory: "What is positively dangerous is to give up the quest for truth about the past and instead to celebrate multiple, incompatible stories about the past, thus suggesting that no story corresponds

---

[3] Marc Gopin, *Holy War, Holy Peace: How Religion Can Bring Peace to the Middle East* (New York: Oxford University Press, 2002), 7.

more accurately to actual events than the other."[4] In this chapter, nonetheless, I am not advocating giving credence to every unrelated story about this or that event. Moreover, I am sympathetic to Volf's concerns and believe to some extent being about borders involves researching the stories, memories, and feelings of all the parties at the border. At the same time, it needs to be admitted that all conversation is enacted in emotionally charged social contexts that in turn shape one's reading of one another's story. As close to the facts that one party attempts to keep their story, it might be received quite differently depending on the other person's mood or predicament. Without a doubt, emotions move and affect our stories, complicating border life. Attempting to learn about the other from listening to their stories without vigilance to one another's emotional needs is potentially futile, since one's reception of another's story is influenced by one another's desires. It is not that all stories are equally valid or true; rather, in attempting to live out affective openness to others, one is chosen to reflect on how various stories overlap and intertwine with one another and how one's feelings about what happened are at times just as important as the facts.

Getting the story straight about public events or illustrious histories is challenging because the ways in which they are narrated are often enmeshed in layers of media spin. Stories about deeply disturbing visceral issues, such as injury, war, or even death can complicate the quest for truth. In "How to Tell a True War Story," Tim O'Brien brings to light the ineffability of expressing war: "Sometimes it's just beyond telling."[5] When someone does try to convey the story, they are forced to manufacture events and feelings for the sake of credibility: "Often the crazy stuff [about war] is true and the normal stuff isn't, because the normal stuff is necessary to make you believe the truly incredible craziness."[6] In attending to gripping plots involving global conflicts, it might prove more beneficial to relinquish an ideal of the truth altogether and instead to opt for the story that feels most urgent.

Given my preliminary remarks it should not sound strange for me to claim that the labels of "Israeli" and "Palestinian" are as much a product of our public and global emotional needs as of our knowledge of the

---

[4] Miroslav Volf, *The End of Memory: Remembering Rightly in a Violent World* (Grand Rapids, MI: Eerdmans Publishing Company, 2006), 57.

[5] Tim O'Brien, "How to Tell a True War Story," in *The Things They Carried* (Boston: Houghton Mifflin, 1990), 79.

[6] Ibid.

truth. Much like the storytelling regarding Edith Stein, uncovering the "one true story" about Israeli or Palestinian identity is in all probability impossible; still, analyzing how characters of each community are shaped by many of the cultural images and trends in the world's political landscape is feasible and indeed necessary. Moreover, even though modern-day Israelis and Palestinians might not recognize themselves in these images and characterizations, being about borders depends on acknowledging how any of the roles we play, fabricated or factual, or more likely somewhere in-between, influence how others relate to us and how we relate to others on a visceral and emotional level. Only when we are attentive to how our identities are constrained by certain images and roles and framed by static binaries of good versus evil and victim versus perpetrator are we freed up to let go of and mourn any one story about ourselves that prevents us from opening to right relationships with others. It is my hope that, by scrutinizing how these characters of the Middle East are placed in relation to stories about the land that many call holy, others who are serious about being about borders, like Christians in the United States after 9/11, can begin to question the types of roles they play in global relationships and begin to reimagine for what or for whom they are chosen.

Character Development

While unrelenting media coverage of developments in the Middle East may create a context in which the characters of the Israelis and the Palestinians seem to have been around for centuries, most experts place the historical emergence of their identities quite recently.[7] The Palestinian story began to unfold in its current form, publicly, in 1947 when the United Nations determined the fate of those residing in the region of Palestine by partitioning it into two states, one Arab and one Jewish, with Jerusalem serving as an international city. This resulted in attacks on several Israelis by Palestinians, beginning what is called by some the War for Israeli Independence and by others, specifically the Palestinian Arabs, *al-Nakba*, meaning "the Catastrophe." As both parties developed different ways to name and frame the events around the tumultuous days of May 1948 and Israeli statehood, competing stories with opposing characters began to emerge.

---

[7] For a concise account of the events leading up to the Israeli-Palestinian crisis and the emergence of their respective identities, see La Guardia, *War Without End*, 377–81.

The month prior to Israel becoming a state was a pivotal period in the character development of the Palestinian. On April 9, 1948, over one hundred Palestinian Arabs in the village of Deir Yassin were massacred by commandos of the extremist Zionist groups known as Irgun and the Stern Gang, precipitating the mass exile of roughly seven hundred thousand Palestinian Arabs from their homes and setting the stage for the world to regard these alienated people as refugees.[8] Nonetheless, the view of the Palestinian as refugee did not last for long. As Israel's borders changed so did the portrayal of the Palestinian, shifting from refugee to the role of the desperate and primitive insurgent. La Guardia captures this transformation of image as he reports on the experiences of a senior military commander and political activist, Salah Ta'mari, who was drawn into the Palestinian struggle after the losses to Israel in the Six Day War (1967). Here is a snapshot of Ta'mari's reflections: "'Our world was turned upside down. Our dreams were shattered in just a few hours,' explained Ta'mari. 'I dropped out of Cairo University in my final year and picked up a gun. I became a full-timer of Al-Asifa, the military wing of Fatah. Had things not gone the way they did in 1967 I would never have thought of joining the military. I wanted to stay in Bethlehem where I lived. I wanted to become a teacher, a writer maybe. Most of us who picked up a gun were more an intelligentsia in khaki than primitive people who did not know any better.'"[9] As one can see, the roles from which Ta'mari had to choose and the one in which he ultimately was cast did not fit his sense of self, story, and place.

Like in any global drama, shifts in images and roles of both individuals and groups are influenced by geopolitical happenings. Each of Israel's gains required an increase in its security measures, exacerbating the tensions between the Israelis and the Palestinians and leaving the Palestinians with what some argue to be a choice of either being swallowed up by the Israelis or "mak[ing] themselves so indigestible to Israelis that they want to disgorge them into their own state."[10] By choosing the latter and refusing to participate in the Israeli system of trade and law to the extent of causing violence, the first uprising or *intifada* in 1987 made the public statement that "[w]e are not you," that the Palestinians are separate

---

[8] For more on the history of Deir Yassin and how it relates to Israeli-Palestinian politics, see Daniel McGowan and Marc H. Ellis, eds., *Remembering Deir Yassin: The Future of Israel and Palestine* (Brooklyn: Olive Branch Press, 1998).

[9] LaGuardia, *War Without End*, 139.

[10] Thomas L. Friedman, *From Beirut to Jerusalem*, Updated with a New Chapter (New York: Random House, 1995), 421.

and distinct from the Israelis.[11] The character type of the Palestinian shifted yet again, morphing from that of the primitive insurgent to an even worse type, the terrorist. Echoing sentiments regarding the family metaphor previously discussed, Eliakim Haetzni, one of the "outspoken ideologues of the settlement movement," frames the development of the image of the Palestinian sharply: "Zionism created a conscience among Arabs who call themselves Palestinian. It's a son born out of wedlock. It happens to the best of families."[12] This is the son who publicly displays all sorts of extreme emotions, frequently causing an embarrassing scene. As stories about the Palestinians continued to shift, the world started to view the Palestinians more like reckless troublemakers than downtrodden refugees or what some have called primitive insurgents.

Today, many have moved to recast the Palestinian as the underdog, the victim of Israeli politics, rather than as the perpetrator of terror. These shifts in public image demonstrate how the portrayals of both parties, the Israelis and the Palestinians, are dependent on the stories, memories, and feelings of one another as well as those of other communities throughout the world. In the early days of Israeli statehood, Jewish settlers were portrayed innocently as refugees from a history plagued by dehumanization and suffering. This representation of the Israeli has had staying power, surfacing in claims that Israel is not a colonizing power but a state that emerged from settler immigrants as they clashed with the indigenous population.[13] At the same time, it is not uncommon for Israelis to be illustrated as colonizers, the ones responsible for the desperation of the Palestinian people. For example, Norman Finkelstein in *Image and Reality of the Israel-Palestine Conflict* attests that the idea that Palestine was settled by Jews rather than colonized by them is one of the many myths in the enduring struggle for the Holy Land.[14] Changes to the description of the Israeli can be traced, according to Thomas Friedman, to when Israel invaded Lebanon in 1982. As gruesome acts of violence were reported, American Jews in particular became increasingly less proud and more skeptical of the goals of Zionism. Friedman frames changing American attitudes toward Israel in terms of a romantic fling:

[11] Ibid., 380.

[12] La Guardia, *War Without End*, 280, 281.

[13] See Ran Greenstein, *Genealogies of Conflict: Class, Identity, and State in Palestine/Israel and South Africa* (Hanover, NH: University Press of New England, 1995).

[14] Norman G. Finkelstein, *Image and Reality of the Israel-Palestine Conflict*, 2nd rev. ed. (London: Verso, 2003).

"Although Israelis and American Jews began dating and fell in love after 1967, they never got married; they never made that total commitment to each other."[15]

There is an epic-like and apocalyptic tone to the Israeli-Palestinian conflict that influences how each character is developed and is perceived—a drama between good and evil where who or what is good or evil is constantly shifting. An end to the violence in the Middle East would seem to require careful attention to the conflicting images and symbols that mediate the disputed narratives of both parties. Until both parties and the rest of the world are honest about the ways in which images of each group are used as propaganda to indirectly express deeper fears and anxieties, the violence will continue. In other words, for a meaningful relationship to emerge, we all must acknowledge the semiotic discontinuities within these stories about Israeli and Palestinian identity and risk exposure by conveying the fears and anxieties present in any dialogue open to the stories, memories, and feelings of the other. Publicly processing the stories about self and other is precisely what being about borders calls for in order to thwart any further narcissistic dehumanization of individuals or groups.

PLAYING THE ROLE OF VICTIM

Suffering is a key theme in much of the literature on Palestinian and Israeli identity, since at one point or another in their stories they both have been cast as victims. For the Palestinian, the notion of suffering at the hands of the world in general and the Israeli militant in particular frames their history, first being cast as the refugee, then the terrorist, and now what some might describe as the oppressed. For Israelis, however, suffering is often tied to arguments for the land. In the beginning of Israel's history they were framed as innocent victims, then as survivors of continuing aggression, and now what some might describe as high-tech terrorists.

Being typed in the role or claiming the role of the victim can turn deadly as narcissistic rationalizations lead to all sorts of violent actions against others. For instance, some have argued that the fear of being victimized allowed many in the world to ignore the Palestinians who were being tortured and murdered in Lebanese refugee camps during

---

[15] Friedman, *From Beirut to Jerusalem*, 461.

the Lebanese Civil War: "The Israeli soldiers did not see innocent civilians being massacred and they did not hear the screams of innocent children going to their graves. What they saw was a 'terrorist infestation' being 'mopped up' and 'terrorist nurses' scurrying about and 'terrorist teenagers' trying to defend them, and what they heard were 'terrorist women' screaming. In the Israeli psyche you don't come to the rescue of 'terrorists.' There is no such thing as 'terrorists' being massacred."[16] It is really difficult to break out of the role in which someone has been typecast. As long as Palestinians, or any others for that matter, are unilaterally typed as terrorists they cannot be acknowledged as flesh-and-blood human beings with particular stories, memories, and feelings that need to be heeded. In U.S. politics, this has been part of the challenge of dealing with the brutality against prisoners at Abu Ghraib, for if we do not consider the prisoners as human, then it is all the more difficult to understand them as victims of torture and our inhumanity.

It is significant to note that pro-Palestinian discourse hinges on playing the role of victim as well and not allowing for the others, meaning the Israelis, to be seen as victims. It is not unusual to hear that the actions taken against the Arab refugees who were forced to leave their homes were analogous to crimes of "ethnic cleansing" and even that life under Israeli occupation is akin to being in a concentration camp.[17] In *Holy War, Holy Peace*, Marc Gopin claims that such analogies about suffering employed by either the Israelis or the Palestinians are unhelpful because they create confusion between "manufactured injury" and "actual injury."[18] For Gopin, actual injury refers to verifiable trauma suffered by an individual or group that influences the development of their identity, such as rape or torture, while manufactured injury points to the situation in which political forces exploit the trauma of some to create an identity for all around that trauma. Implicit in Gopin's argument is the conviction that not all suffering is the same. While his concerns are definitely important for those interested in what really happened, there are those who are called to be about borders no matter what happened. Gopin acknowledges this, arguing that dismissing manufactured injury is not always possible or just: "[W]hether individuals or groups search for misery in order to discover identity, or whether political leaders manufacture injury, it does not mean that this misery is not real to the people who feel

[16] Ibid., 163.
[17] La Guardia, *War Without End*, 186.
[18] Gopin, *Holy War, Holy Peace*, 96–97.

it. Thus, whatever its roots, injuries must be confronted and accepted by the highest levels of diplomacy and conflict resolution practice, although it would be helpful for groups to go through an honest process of historical examination on these matters."[19] Considering Gopin's comments, for any other relationship than one imbued with violence to emerge between the Israelis and the Palestinians, stories about hurt and injustice need to be sorted. As with the case of the canonization of Edith Stein, usurping the other's story and thereby manufacturing injury only results in destroying the alterity of the other. Conversely, being about borders must allow for ambiguity in storytelling, memory, and feeling—for the porosity of borders. To be sure, not all feelings can be clinically diagnosed in terms of trauma; however, does it necessarily follow that the individual or group experiencing negative manufactured feelings be denied empathy and care because manufactured feelings do not deserve to be acknowledged?

In gearing up for conflict and exposure at the borders one is called to sift through actual and manufactured injury and consequently the rhetorically charged portrayals of self, story, and place. This process may demand that the world begin to recognize the Palestinians as a distinct people as opposed to inhuman terrorists. It also may require that the world resist turning its back on Israel and demonizing them as the latest terrorists. Additionally, it may be necessary to admit that differentiating real from manufactured injury is difficult, if not impossible, that moving and mixing at the borders, that is, hybridity, has already occurred, and that at some point or another we have all felt like terrorists, acted the part, or been cast in the role.

Memory and Story

As already mentioned in connection with Jewish-Catholic relations, one's perspective on injury relates to their re-membering and their storytelling. Friedman argues this exact point when he claims that many have experienced Auschwitz as a life-changing event, which has given way to a specific type of storytelling, one that he calls "Yad Vasheming," in which every aspect of life is framed through the narrative memory of the Shoah.[20] According to Friedman, since the atrocities of the Shoah are

[19] Ibid.
[20] Friedman, *From Beirut to Jerusalem*, 282.

commemorated by the Yad Vashem memorial in Jerusalem and are attended by Israeli schoolchildren and many visitors, the psychological fear of being a victim has come to permeate the Israeli worldview, leading to the "'Holocausting' of the Israeli psyche, actually encourag[ing] it, turning the Palestinians into the new Nazis and Israel into a modern-day Warsaw Ghetto aligned against the world."[21] Friedman's comments regarding Yad Vashem are undoubtedly difficult for many to hear as they interrupt the dominant narrative about the Israeli story and identity as one as a result of unwarranted oppression and persecution by the other. Nonetheless, they are worth noting as they clearly illuminate how affect influences memory which in turn impacts the stories we tell about ourselves and others.

In analyzing the impact of Yad Vashem, Friedman is hinting at the pathological effects of human memory, when our feelings shape the way we remember and tell our story to the point of the exclusion of the other. Romanticizing characters or mislabeling pivotal events within the story have the potential to obscure the complexity of border life, not allowing for complicated feelings to be grappled with and quite possibly for solidarity among disparate groups of victims to emerge. This is the situation that Volf wants to avoid when he speaks of remembering for the good of the larger community. Some have argued however that attaching the notion of pathology to the process of remembering is problematic because it undermines the momentous role that memory serves in human existence. Paul Ricoeur worries about undercutting the importance of memory and argues that "we have nothing better than memory to signify that something has taken place."[22] Instead of giving up on memory altogether, it might prove more beneficial to re-member in a fashion that is ready for conflict and open to exposure in relation to another's stories. Being about borders means taking all our stories regarding difference seriously and trying to deal with the emotionally charged issues that caused them or at the very least surround them.

Volf characterizes this complex call to deal with one another's stories, memories, and feelings as a "journey," which "follows the path that starts with remembering truthfully, condemning wrong deeds, healing inner wounds, releasing wrongdoers from punishment and guilt, repentance by and transformation of wrongdoers, and reconciliation between the

---

[21] Ibid., 280.

[22] Paul Ricoeur, *Memory, History, Forgetting*, trans. Kathleen Blamey and David Pellauer (Chicago: University of Chicago Press, 2004), 21.

wronged and their wrongdoers; and it ends with the letting go of the memory of wrongdoing."[23] As the journey of re-membering begins with conflict and exposure, it culminates in a process of relinquishment and mourning. This type of re-membering admits hybridity, that we are all made up of many stories, some of which overlap and intertwine with another, and begins to embrace a life of emotional homelessness. Instead of wielding the posture that screams, "That's my story and I'm sticking to it!" we are chosen to admit by re-membering that there are other stories to be heard, some of which connect with and contest our own. This type of intimate storytelling and listening with the other is necessary in being about borders. In *The Call of Stories*, Robert Coles highlights this precise sentiment as he remembers what physician and poet William Carlos Williams had once told him about the significance of stories in human relationships: "'We have to pay the closest attention to what we say. What patients say tells us what to think about what hurts them; and what we say tells us what is happening to us—what we are thinking, and what may be wrong with us.' . . . 'Their story, yours, mine—it's what we all carry with us on this trip we take, and we owe it to each other to respect our stories and learn from them.'"[24]

For Whom or What Are We Chosen?

So far I have argued that being about borders in a global context not only demands keen attention to how stereotypes are constructed in the world's imagination and to the power of communal memory but also depends on a larger vision, namely, that of being open to the call of another's story. We are chosen to be for the other through heeding their feelings, memories, and stories. Chosenness is a complex notion. Already I have alluded to the importance of being chosen for the other at borders in my previous discussions of interpersonal and interreligious life. Here, I further develop that sense of chosenness by emphasizing its religious undertones. When understood in this fullest sense, chosenness has the potential to take on a more meaningful and fulfilling role in the opera of our everyday lives, as a summons to open to the barrage of emotions that otherness brings.

---

[23] Volf, *The End of Memory*, 151.

[24] Robert Coles, *The Call of Stories: Teaching and the Moral Imagination* (Boston: Houghton Mifflin Company, 1989), 30.

Before underscoring the religious sense of chosenness, it is worth noting that chosenness is part of so many of our everyday experiences and is felt in conflicting ways, in that at the same time as it connotes a sense of privilege, it is imbued with a sense of obligation. When it develops as privilege, the individual or group is regarded as special and thereby entitled to unique opportunities. Alternatively, when it manifests as obligation, chosenness wields the potential to foster a type of being about borders in which individuals and groups act charitably toward one another at a cost to themselves. Someone cast as the "special one" is challenged to deal with both the privileged and obligatory facets of their new role. For example, when a student becomes the "teacher's pet," they usually acquire certain perks, such as being allowed more freedom or creativity than other students in the classroom. Many of us have heard that there is no such thing as a free lunch. In this hypothetical scenario the instructor might expect something extra from the student, such as consistently achieving outstanding grades. If and when either party fails to live up to the other's expectation, the relationship could fall apart.

More relevant to this study, aspects of being elected into relationship manifest either explicitly or implicitly in all the Abrahamic religions in that they all vie for being named as legitimate heirs to God's affection and inheritance, creating a contested legacy that was explored in the previous chapter. To be sure, in Jewish contexts, chosenness is a dominant theme, with clear scriptural links between being chosen and having rights to land: "For you are a people holy to the Lord your God; the Lord your God has chosen you out of all the peoples on earth to be his people, his treasured possession" (Deut 7:6); "And because he loved your ancestors, he chose their descendants after them. He brought you out of Egypt with his own presence, by his great power, driving out before you nations greater and mightier than yourselves, to bring you in, giving you their land for a possession, as it is still today" (Deut 4:37-38). Claims about the "sacred myth of chosenness" can be found in Jewish ritual as well: "The religious festivals—Passover, Shavuot, Sukkot, and the Holy Days, Rosh Hashanah, and Yom Kippur—start with the blessing over wine, which begins: 'Blessed are You, Lord our God, King of the universe, who has chosen us from among every nation, exalted us above every language, and sanctified us by Your commandments.' "[25]

---

[25] David S. Ariel, *What Do Jews Believe? The Spiritual Foundations of Judaism* (New York: Schocken Books, 1995), 114.

Christianity has its own rendition of chosenness, which is not understood so much as being entitled to land but rather as being chosen for the spiritual inheritance of salvation. Most problematically, some Christians reread the election of Israel as the precursor to their own: "As the Christian church became more Gentile and more institutionalized, it came to see itself more as a new elect *historical* community, superseding a morally and spiritually inferior historical community of the Jews."[26] By this point, it probably is obvious that if one is serious about being about borders, one is called to question these types of sentiments and decide whether being singled out as special leads to chauvinism, in which the election of one party at the border ultimately leads to the rejection of the others.

Contrary to the references to being chosen in Judaism and Christianity, for Muslims, Islam is an offer for all, an idea frequently referred to as the "universal appeal" of Islam: "Acceptance into the Islamic fold is not limited to Arabs, some chosen people, or a particular nation or tribe. Islam rises above race, ethnicity, gender, color, nationality, social standing, and other narrow considerations. It is also not restricted to any period of time. The message delivered by Muhammad is supposed to be final and, hence, eternal."[27] Nonetheless, in Islam, one still can detect references to ties to the land that many call holy. There is a sense that both Jews and Christians have forfeited their rights to any divine inheritance by not being faithful to Allah. From the many references to him in the Qurʾan, it is clear that Islam considers Moses a worthy prophet; nonetheless, there is the conviction that when, according to the Hebrew Scriptures, the Israelites disregarded God's order to enter into the Promised Land in fear of not being able to survive there, they unwittingly relinquished all claims to the land. Moreover, when the Lord banished the Israelites into the wilderness for forty years, "God's promise was cancelled."[28] According to the Qurʾan, the Israelites' loss is the Muslims' gain; as a result of their fidelity, Muslims have been offered both the land and Allah's favor: "Allah has promised, to those among you who believe

---

[26] Rosemary Radford Ruether and Herman J. Ruether, *The Wrath of Jonah: The Crisis of Religious Nationalism in the Israeli-Palestinian Conflict*, 2nd ed. (Minneapolis: Fortress Press, 2002), 25.

[27] Arshad Khan, *Islam, Muslims, and America: Understanding the Basis of Their Conflict* (New York: Algora Publishing, 2003), 139–40.

[28] La Guardia, *War Without End*, 57. For scriptural background on this narrative event, see Num 13:32–14:35.

and work righteous deeds, that He will, of a surety, grant them in the land, inheritance (of power), as He granted it to those before them; that He will establish in authority their religion—the one which He has chosen for them; and that He will change (their state), after the fear in which they (lived), to one of security and peace: 'They will worship Me (alone) and not associate anything with Me.' If any do reject Faith after this, they are rebellious and wicked."[29]

Some Muslims, particularly those associated with Hamas (the Islamic Resistance Movement), think Palestine is "a *waqf,* or Islamic endowment, a sacred possession given in perpetuity. There can never be another sovereignty, and Muslims are duty-bound to fight Israel."[30] This notion was formalized in the controversial Hamas Covenant that was devised in 1988: "The Islamic Resistance Movement believes that the land of Palestine has been an Islamic Waqf throughout the generations and until the Day of Resurrection, no one can renounce it or part of it, or abandon it or part of it. . . . Any demarche in violation of this law of Islam, with regard to Palestine, is baseless and reflects on its perpetrators."[31]

As there are clearly too many threads in the Abrahamic traditions related to election to elaborate on here, it might help to hone in on one tradition in an effort to move toward conceptualizing chosenness as charity, as an impetus to being open to all the affective disturbances of border life, both the privilege and obligation of it. By exploring a handful of the more specific Jewish appropriations of chosenness, in what follows I aim to provide a framework for those committed to being about borders, including those thinking about the Israeli-Palestinian conflict as well as those invested in rethinking what it means to be human after 9/11.

CHOSEN FOR LIFE AT THE BORDERS

Judaism presents a strong tradition of thinking through chosenness, and some interpretations are more amenable than others to our conversation on being about borders. In much of the literature on election, one does not have much control over the circumstances of their being chosen. Judah Halevi, a medieval philosopher and poet, supported this perspec-

---

[29] The Qur'an 24:55, trans. Abdullah Yusaf Ali (Elmhurst, NY: Tahrike Tarsile Qur'an, Inc., 2006).

[30] La Guardia, *War Without End,* 56.

[31] See The Charter of Allah: The Platform of the Islamic Resistance Movement (Hamas), 1988, http://www.palestinecenter.org/cpap/documents/charter.html (accessed October 7, 2007).

tive as he upheld an ontological reading of chosenness in which being special was part of one's biological makeup. In his *Kuzari*, Halevi explains chosenness as being a gift from God in which Jews are bestowed a particular and supernatural quality that marks Israel as a species that is separate and distinct from other groups. Accordingly, God endows Israel with a "religious faculty" that is particular to them through the inheritance of Adam.[32] Here chosenness manifests as an innate dimension of Jewish being that distinguishes Jews from others and predisposes them to both privilege and obligation, and notably obligation is one of the key aspects in being about borders.

In contrast to this essentialist and ontological reading, chosenness can also be interpreted as the result of socialization and practice, not of one's nature but as a result of one being nurtured in a specific way. Historically, Moses Maimonides has been categorized as maintaining this sense of chosenness in which being a member of Israel is dependent not on being born with a certain biology but rather, on the contrary, on living out the Torah. Menachem Kellner explains: "Consistent with his philosophical psychology, Maimonides develops a theory of ethics according to which human beings at birth are *tabulae rasae*, upon which education, training, and acculturation write out our moral characters. . . . Obedience to the Torah leads to high moral virtue; in this sense Jews, Maimonides held, are morally superior to Gentiles. But that is a matter of education, not inborn character."[33] Other Jewish thinkers have echoed Maimonides' perspective, including Mordecai Kaplan. Working within a Jewish reconstructionist framework, Kaplan asserts that being chosen is not about God finding favor with a people but about God granting Jews the "opportunity" to experience his call by working within and for a specific culture and developing it into a "civilization" through the cultivation of land, language, aesthetics, and religion.[34]

---

[32] Henry Slonimsky, introduction to *The Kuzari: An Argument for the Faith of Israel*, by Judah Halevi (New York: Schocken Books, 1964), 28.

[33] Menachem Kellner, "Chosenness, Not Chauvinsm: Maimonides on the Chosen People," in *A People Apart: Chosenness and Ritual in Jewish Philosophical Thought*, ed. Daniel H. Frank (Albany: SUNY Press, 1993), 55.

[34] Mordecai M. Kaplan, *Judaism as a Civilization: Toward a Reconstruction of American-Jewish Life* (New York: Schocken Books, 1967), 258. See also Kaplan, *The Future of the American Jew* (New York: Reconstructionist Press, 1967); and *The Religion of Ethical Nationhood: Judaism's Contribution to World Peace* (London: The Macmillan Company, 1970).

Eugene Borowitz emphasizes similar ethical dimensions of chosenness to that of Maimonides and Kaplan. Nevertheless, he avoids the individualistic manifestations, which are bound up with the thought of modernity. Mapping the dual nature of chosenness as both intracommunal and extracommunal in which Jews simultaneously are called into a distinct holy life from all others through living out Torah and are obligated to engage others in all their diversity through service, Borowitz expands the reading of chosenness to encompass a postmodern sensitivity to otherness, specifically to the complex stories of other religious traditions.[35] In attempting to be open to those outside of the Jewish tradition, he privileges the notion of covenant over chosenness since covenant better captures the relational affinities necessary for flourishing in a pluralist context. His analysis provides the foundation for a being about borders that is vigilant about the other's stories, memories, and feelings in addition to one's own.

All of these dimensions are significant for an anthropology of difference, yet Marc H. Ellis is arguably a Jewish thinker most purposeful about framing chosenness in terms of an openness to others. Regarding Israeli-Palestinian relations, he claims that "The new challenge of the covenant is to find Jewish chosenness within and among those who share the land often called Holy."[36] Rethinking the connection between chosenness and suffering, Ellis even asserts that Auschwitz will only end when Israelis and Palestinians recognize themselves in one another. Instead of invoking the Shoah to secure Israel's boundaries he employs it as a bridge for creating empathy for the Palestinian other. As one might imagine his ideas are controversial and counterintuitive that in times of great suffering, the Babylonian Exile, Masada, the Crusades, the Inquisition, and the Shoah, "chosenness was the promise that made the unbearable bearable."[37]

Ellis's reading of border life with the Palestinians resists the impulse to frame chosenness in light of victimization and consequently avoids any narcissistic expression of it. His intent is not to dismiss the feelings of trauma experienced by Jewish communities worldwide after the Shoah but rather to provide a model of existence for overcoming trauma by

---

[35] Eugene B. Borowitz, *Renewing the Covenant: A Theology for the Postmodern Jew* (Philadelphia: The Jewish Publication Society, 1991), 195.

[36] Marc H. Ellis, *O, Jerusalem! The Contested Future of the Jewish Covenant* (Minneapolis: Fortress Press, 1999), 86.

[37] W. Gunther Plaut, *The Case for the Chosen People* (Garden City, NY: Doubleday & Company, Inc., 1965), 137.

breaking out of the cycle of victimization and engaging the stories, memories, and feelings of the other. His reading of chosenness unequivo- cally demands an engagement of others, electing each one of us for a life at the borders. In this short section, we see how important thinking through chosenness manifests for a particular community. Ultimately, in imagining being about borders for a global world and as post-9/11 global tensions continue to fester, it is not too strong to suggest that Christians in the United States have the occasion, opportunity, and obli- gation to evaluate how they live with others at the borders and to grapple with the question of for whom or for what are they chosen, a life of charity or entitlement, incorporating Ellis's bold and courageous reading of chosenness into their own lives.

Applying Lessons Learned to the U.S. Context

For Christians in the United States, being about borders must mean being vigilant about the other's needs, feelings, memories, and stories. To do this, acknowledging, respecting, and managing the affective dis- sonance that accompanies hybrid existence must become one's priority. In a way, emotion for another is what calls us into being. While thinking and acting are essential aspects of maintaining a relationship with an- other, it is the affective disturbance that emerges in the encounter with another that first elects us into a relationship of being. Being open and exposing oneself to the risk-filled and dangerous terrain of an emotion- ally charged relationship with another requires, like those embroiled in the Israeli-Palestinian crises, a commitment to listen to another's story, including the way characters, stories, and themes are developed. In this particular moment in the United States, in a culture that breeds a narcis- sistic avoidance of limits, Christians challenging themselves to be about borders need to be open to the possibility that there might not be one pure story or that they may not be able to get the story straight about the characters and events that define the time. More strongly put, for those who are living in the midst of terrorism and have been elected to live as Jesus did with an other-oriented style and with a reverence for the mystery of the incarnation, embracing their hybrid selves and relin- quishing any and all stories of purity and innocence must become every- day happenings.

Incarnating hybridity with an eye toward theological claims about borders and difference undoubtedly means getting prepared for conflict with one another since few are willing to cease conceptualizing terrorism through the binary of good versus evil. It also entails telling and hence exposing one's story to the world, not only in terms of being the victim after 9/11, but also in light of the possibility of being the victimizer. Finally, being about borders in the United States implies that some notions of self, story, and place must be given up for the sake of others at the borders. This is probably the most difficult aspect of being about borders because it requires one to act on feelings, that is to say, not only to feel empathy for the other, but more than that, to change one's life because of the other's suffering.

Storytelling after 9/11

After 9/11, many U.S. citizens, and many of them Christian, have adhered to a certain image when identifying themselves: the victim. Feeling victimized by terrorists who can be anyone and can strike anywhere at any time has led to unending discourse and anxiety about the need to survive in this uncertain world, reflecting the narcissistic attitude discussed earlier.[38] These fears over survival can have disastrous effects in that as long as individuals or cultures perceive themselves as the injured party they will do anything to secure their safety. It is a situation analogous to what Friedman writes about in terms of the Israeli-Palestinian conflict: "The Jews have been standing on the subway of life for two thousand years. One day in 1948, they finally got a seat."[39] The fear of losing that seat and falling victim again becomes paralyzing because it is contextualized in a past trauma or an unhealed wound. Giving up one's seat symbolizes giving up one's security: "Someone who sees himself as a victim will almost never morally evaluate himself or put limits on his own actions. Why should he? He is the victim."[40] So burdened by anxieties about their well-being, those who have suffered from events surrounding 9/11, like weary commuters, begin to ignore or, even worse, become anesthetized to the needs and feelings of others.

Beginning to be about borders in the midst of the affective overflow of 9/11, including that related to the U.S. military engagements around the world, requires great courage and stamina in order to analyze how

---

[38] For more on the connection between narcissism and anxieties about survival, see Christopher Lasch, *The Minimal Self: Psychic Survival in Troubled Times* (New York: W.W. Norton & Company, 1984).

[39] Friedman, *From Beirut to Jerusalem*, 407.

[40] Ibid., 144.

the roles of victim and perpetrator are cast and consider whether, and if so how, the stories about the victims and the perpetrators overlap and intertwine. These character types in the current geopolitical context have been so heavily typecast that there is very little wiggle room in the public sphere to imagine the roles as overlapping, that the one who has been hurt may be connected to those who are responsible for causing the injury. In other words, like within the stalemate between the Israelis and the Palestinians, there is limited tolerance for embracing hybrid existence within the backdrop of global fears about terrorism.

For some it may seem ludicrous to cast the United States, a nation often touted as one of the greatest superpowers in the world, in the role of victim, as an entity in trouble. All the same, public testimonies about the 9/11 attacks and aftermath have created precisely this character type. And on some level, if one wants to employ Gopin's argument, this makes sense. An event in which ordinary people die at the hands of others who transgressed international, technological, and some might argue religious borders in violence represents an instance of actual injury. On another level, the shock and trauma-like feelings around these events have prevented many from inquiring about why this happened and from reading how their own individual or national stories lead to this sort of transgression, in other words from dealing with any manufactured injury. Since 9/11 there has been little public acceptance of being about borders, of recognizing the other's pain, suffering, and, most important for our purposes, feelings, which may or may not have led up to the attacks or to the pervasive military presence of U.S. troops around the world. Instead, there has been a pathological patrolling of borders all in the name of survival. In proposing being about borders as an anthropology that engages difference within the interpersonal, interreligious, and international realms of everyday life, Christians must resist any sort of patriotism based in the ideology of victimhood and grapple with the emotionally loaded stories of others, even the stories of those typed as perpetrators. This is the same type of risk that Ellis chances when he rethinks covenant and chosenness in the midst of the Israeli-Palestinian crisis.

Even if implicitly, 9/11 has brought the question of chosenness to the forefront of life in the United States. The wave of media coverage of anti-American rallies throughout the world and of the publicized link between the United States and Israel has stirred not only anti-Arab violence but also the resurgence of anti-Jewish sentiment. By rethinking chosenness and even being critical of some appropriations of it, I am not attempting to reinscribe such stereotypes or incite more anxiety; instead,

I am endeavoring to advance a more life-giving way of being human in the global arena. Neither naïve nor idealistic, I realize that exposing one's anxieties about self, story, and place after 9/11 is perilous. One chances being labeled treasonous or blasphemous or, even worse, of being accused of disrespecting those who were injured or killed in their efforts to resist terrorism. Nevertheless, by incarnating human existence that is grounded in vigilance about the emotional complexity of our hybrid existence, Christians have an ethical obligation to work at getting ready for conflict, exposing their fears, and embracing mourning as they retell their stories.

Mourning in the Global Landscape

While the gospels and doctrinal teachings related to hybridity and difference underscore what is at stake in being about borders, there are no instructions for how to handle the emotional messiness of living at the borders within the global landscape where cultures and religions have such seemingly disparate worldviews. When one encounters a portrait of Jesus who eats with the tax collectors, associates with women we now would call the marginalized, and demonstrates other acts of solidarity at the borders, one is left wondering what kind of visceral reaction he may have experienced in relation to their otherness, and if and how he worked through it. Did he feel dirty and want to bathe after meeting with women? Did dining with others make him feel ill at ease and even leave him with an upset stomach? The gospel stories about Jesus do not deal with these very real and often debilitating corporeal reactions to those who are different. This omission is not reason enough to avoid the affective disturbances of relating to others. Moreover, until Christians deal with their own affective dissonance in relation to their partners, neighbors, or enemies, fulfilling the gospel call to live with others at the borders will be a futile undertaking.

This corporeal dimension of living with others is nothing to be embarrassed about since we all have stories, memories, and emotions that make us feel physically and emotionally uncomfortable. Denying this fact risks renouncing one's humanity and consequently repudiating the very existence that God deems sacred enough to incarnate in the first place. If one embraces the gravity of the incarnation, that God was "enfleshed in a body that ate and drank, slept and woke, touched and received touch," then by living in the footsteps of Jesus one is unequivocally called to deal with the conflicting feelings associated with this corporeal existence.[41] The problem therefore is not with the presence of conflicting stories, memories, and feelings that arise when encountering others, but with holding on to them at the expense of another's visceral stories, memories, and feelings.

It follows that in order to be about borders in the global context, Christians, and here I am speaking about those in the United States, are chosen not only to embrace their own conflicting, embodied feelings of hurt but also, like Jesus, to include those of another. They must be other-oriented and hence ready to listen to the other's story no matter how painful, off-putting, or ridiculous it may seem, and they must be willing to eventually let go and mourn feelings of hurt before they cause more potentially deadly border actions. Accepting the feelings that challenge one's injury surrounding 9/11 does not dishonor the dead; quite the opposite, it honors them by creating a space for one another's emotions to be felt so they do not fester and cause additional violence. Gopin writes about the dangers of using the dead for the "genesis and perpetuation of conflict."[42] Moreover he is critical of what he calls "perpetuated mourning" or "the state in which human beings find one way or another to keep old wounds open, to keep attachment to the loss by prolonging some state of affairs in which that loss is kept at the surface level of experience, in addition to the perpetuation of moral justification for that position."[43] In being about borders one is chosen to consider that following in the footsteps of Jesus demands raising these sorts of issues about mourning in relation to 9/11 and U.S. military efforts abroad.

Just before the sixth anniversary of 9/11, *The New York Times* ran a piece on the possibility of scaling back memorial events related to those tragic attacks titled "As 9/11 Nears, a Debate Rises: How Much Tribute Is Enough?"[44] As one might expect, there were opposing responses to the inquiry from "doesn't grieving have a shelf life," to "scaling back just seems so offensive." Clearly hurt by the idea that tributes should be limited, one person interviewed referenced the Shoah as a way to frame the magnitude of the 9/11 attacks: "I would no sooner tell survivors of

[41] Stephanie Paulsell, *Honoring the Body: Meditations on a Christian Practice* (San Francisco: Jossey-Bass, 2002), 7.

[42] Gopin, *Holy War, Holy Peace*, 204.

[43] Ibid., 93.

[44] N. R. Kleinfield, "As 9/11 Nears, a Debate Rises: How Much Tribute Is Enough?" *New York Times*, September 2, 2007, 1, *Academic Search Premier*, EBSCOhost (accessed August 24, 2010).

the Holocaust how to mourn or how to commemorate their atrocity, so why do others feel they have any right to dictate how family members should feel or memorialize our loved ones on Sept. 11 or any day, for that matter?" This quote is so powerful because it highlights many of the challenges of being about borders discussed throughout this book: the pitfalls of comparing one injurious event to that of another, the problem of privatizing suffering to such an extreme that some stories and memories are hoarded just for "victimized" individuals and communities, and the challenge of reframing mourning in a way that embraces not just the victim but also the perpetrator. For being about borders to take shape either locally or globally, the act of delving into one another's stories, memories, and feelings about their injury must be interpreted not as an attempt to take away from the emotional impact of another's suffering but more broadly as an act of charity, as being receptive to the feelings of others to the point of recognizing the interconnections between one's sense of self, story, and place and that of another as modeled in creation and the person and work of Christ.

This link between mourning and borders in the global landscape must not be overlooked. Whereas an important component of interpreting Israeli-Palestinian relations is acknowledging the emotional attachment to place, both the physical sense of land and the more abstract sense of position and prestige, in the U.S. context, especially after the devastating attacks of 9/11, one finds a similar preoccupation with place, both literally in the securing of U.S. borders in fear of more attacks and metaphorically in trying to recover from the shock, surprise, and humiliation of one of the world's technological superpowers being overwhelmed by terrorists with limited technological expertise. Citizens of the United States reacted to 9/11 with startling questions. Why do they hate us? How can this happen to such a blessed and chosen nation? How can the United States reclaim its place in the global landscape? For Christians, however, a more charitable line of questioning may be, what's more important for living with others peacefully, to claim place or surrender and mourn it?

Not all rites of mourning 9/11 have been used to promote right relations across borders. Already I have referred to Gopin's work on perpetuated mourning in which one is compelled to remember and grieve an event, such as a mass catastrophe, through organized memorials in order to satisfy their desire for revenge or hatred. It is arguable that the process of "Yad Vasheming" is comparable to what is going on in the United States in a post-9/11 context. It is lurking in the various debates about the right kind of memorial at Ground Zero. It is connected to the constant pressure to remain "patriotic" and "support our troops" in the face of what seems an unending war with a dubious enemy and countless casualties and victims. It is present in the never-ending tributes to those who have perished in or in relation to the attacks on that very tragic day. This is the border challenge for which Christians have been chosen, namely to re-member their stories in relation to one another at the borders so that the telling of those stories around 9/11 does not turn pathological.

Interestingly, Freud also discusses the negative effects of mourning when he addresses the problem of melancholy as a type of mourning gone awry in which the one grieving cannot effectively locate or name what has been lost, in all probability because they have no clear sense of where they end and the other begins. While mourning eventually pushes one to move on, melancholy causes one to become stuck in a narcissistic state, festering "like an open wound."[45] For being about borders to unfold, mourning must overcome the inertia of melancholy.

In comparison to Gopin and Freud, Judith Butler is even more explicit in demonstrating how mourning can be used narcissistically to hold on to security, power, and privilege, particularly in relation to a post-9/11 U.S. setting.[46] For example, she explains how public sentiment allows for only a certain type of mourning, one for the Americans who died in the tragic events on U.S. soil. Mourning anyone or anything other than them seems unacceptable, immoral, and even a betrayal of humanity. This stronghold on how mourning should be expressed after 9/11 reinforces the innocent victim versus evil perpetrator binary, prohibiting any attempt to re-member our stories and embrace hybridity. Being about borders under this type of pressure allows only for securing borders on every level without seeing how they function and what power and privilege they serve. Rather than emulating the mysterious intimacy that Christians proclaim in the incarnation, policed mourning destroys any attempt to embrace the other at the borders.

Christians in the twenty-first century have to move beyond binaries and beyond a simplistic understanding of borders including any interpretation of them that is devoid of their emotional impact. Only then can violent policing borders cease and can genuine and complex

---

[45] Sigmund Freud, "Mourning and Melancholia," in *The Standard Edition of the Complete Psychological Works of Sigmund Freud*, vol. 14, trans. James Strachey (London: The Hogarth Press, 1957), 253.

[46] Judith Butler, *Precarious Life: The Powers of Mourning and Violence* (London: Verso, 2004).

relationships with others emerge. Working toward a Christian under-standing of being human must transcend holding on to what is familiar and encourage being open to the unexpected at the borders. In such an anthropology, Christians are chosen to mourn an idealized self with a pure singular story, in addition to the privilege that allows them to secure that sense of self and story in the first place. Borders become the site of the Christian's ethical obligation to relinquish and to mourn. Only when a more ethical sense of mourning is sustained can Butler's following hopes come to fruition: "I consider our recent trauma [9/11] to be an opportunity for a reconsideration of United States hubris and the im-portance of establishing more radically egalitarian international ties. Doing this involves a certain 'loss' for the country as a whole: the notion of the world itself as the sovereign entitlement of the United States must be given up, lost, and mourned, as narcissistic and grandiose fantasies must be lost and mourned."[47]

In the in-between space between self and other, in the stories of justice and injustice that overlap and intertwine, we find a place to mourn. Guilt or shame finally do not cause this mourning but rather a realization of a loss of privileged self, place, or story when faced with that of another. In living a life of relinquishment we can become memorials to whatever trauma has divided us from one another. Constructing the most impres-sive and state-of-the-art memorials might be the best way to bring heal-ing for some; nevertheless, without mourning our loss of privilege, memorials can also lead to abuses. What better memorial to the injured of humanity is there than being a living, breathing, corporeal sign of many stories, some of which are more just than others, and being willing to admit to them all for the sake of the other?

Reclaiming Diaspora

Recall from the previous chapter that taking another's place can follow two different trajectories, either substituting oneself in order to attend to the needs and feelings of another, or usurping another's possessions, story, or place out of complete disregard for boundaries. Both trajectories unfolded following 9/11. On the one hand, few can forget the images of the heroic efforts of emergency workers at Ground Zero who were will-ing to sacrifice their own well-being in hopes of saving others, or the multitudes at New York City hospitals who stood in line for hours on end so that they could donate their blood for the injured. These are clear

[47] Ibid., 40.

instances of taking the other's place in charity and feeling for one another. On the other hand, amid the endless media attention to what happened, who was hurt, and what kind of memorials should be built, there continues to be a lack of sustained public and popular attention by U.S. citizens to the question of how their country's power and privilege in the world are perceived as threatening to others, or how feelings of entitlement in the United States are strong enough to justify taking the place of others at all costs by hoarding and squandering resources. In light of the traumatic feelings resulting from the fear around terrorism, taking the other's place in charity is only done for those at home, while taking the other's place through entitlement is commonplace at the borders and is even justified by narcissistic anxieties about survival. The question for Christians in the United States is how to reconcile being about borders not just for those individuals and groups with whom they are comfortable but also for the Muslims who are typed as terrorists and who are personally and communally threatened, and perhaps for those immigrants desiring to trespass borders for a better life for their families.

Thinking back to Ellis's work on the obligation associated with chosenness, it might mean that if Christians in the United States are serious about being about borders, about exposing themselves to conflict, vulnerability, and loss in the face of another's feelings, they ought to consider playing the role of the exile, ceasing to guard borders rigorously and even embracing what some call diasporism. For centuries diasporism has been interpreted as a problem, as a temporary state of existence resulting from oppression. According to this perspective, justice prevails when exiles are allowed to return to the place from which they have been alienated. The connotation of diasporism, however, is changing and can alternatively be read in terms of a voluntary homelessness in which one abandons exclusive claims to self, story, and place for the sake of a better relationship with the other.

Brothers Daniel and Jonathan Boyarin in *Powers of Diaspora* give credence to this alternative reading of diaspora existence, arguing implicitly that the imperative to overcome diaspora is part of Western colonialist metanarrative—one that works to squelch difference.[48] Against the

---

[48] Daniel Boyarin and Jonathan Boyarin, *Powers of Diaspora: Two Essays on the Relevance of Jewish Culture* (Minneapolis: University of Minnesota Press, 2002). Their argument poses implications for how one conceptualizes the place of the State of Israel, fostering a reading of Zionism as a Western construct and hence as a form of assimilation. Diasporism for them becomes a formidable mode of Jewish resistance, even a normative way of being Jewish.

assumption that diaspora existence reflects a position of weakness and that citizenship represents a position of power, the Boyarins claim that Jewish identity can only flourish by resisting the hegemony of statehood. In rewriting the diaspora experience as a way to resist the totalizing and violent effects of assimilation, the Boyarins prefigure what I have been referring to as an anthropology of being about borders. Is it plausible that Christians perhaps can follow both Ellis's and the Boyarins' lead, by rejecting displays of entitlement and claims to injury and ultimately becoming comfortable with living the life of an exile?

By this point some might be frustrated with this line of argument: why in the world would anyone willingly take on the role of an exile? Being an exile is not glamorous, especially for those who do not have a home to relinquish in the first place. Moreover, those who have lived as exiles historically are apt to resist my metaphorical reading of it. Edward Said elaborates:

> Against this large, impersonal setting, exile cannot be made to serve notions of humanism. On the twentieth-century scale, exile is neither aesthetically nor humanistically comprehensible: at most the literature about exile objectifies an anguish and a predicament most people rarely experience first hand; but to think of the exile informing this literature as beneficially humanistic is to banalize its mutilations, the losses it inflicts on those who suffer them, the muteness with which it responds to any attempt to understand it as "good for us." Is it not true that the views of exile in literature and, moreover, in religion obscure what is truly horrendous: that exile is irremediably secular and unbearably historical; that it is produced by human beings for other human beings; and that, like death but without death's ultimate mercy, it has torn millions of people from the nourishment of tradition, family and geography?[49]

Said's sobering words challenge the casual use of exile to support anyone's personal or political agenda. Being about borders as a way of dealing with difference in everyday life does not claim to narcissistically appropriate the horrific untranslatable experience of being an outcast, alienated from self, story, and place. Instead, being about borders maintains that individuals and groups, especially those powerful ones, need to renounce exclusive claims to border life, to self, story, and place. Voluntary exile, or what is now referred to as diaspora existence, is the cost of

---

[49] Edward W. Said, "Reflections on Exile," in *Reflections on Exile and Other Essays* (Cambridge, MA: Harvard University Press, 2000), 174.

being about borders—it is the price of being chosen for a life of hybridity, of realizing one's limits as well as the needs, desires, and feelings of another.

It is probably true that most U.S. citizens are not inclined to relinquish their homes or land anytime soon. How, then, is it possible to transform theory into an everyday Christian practice? One of the many important symbols of U.S. culture is the Statue of Liberty, which is inscribed with words of welcome for exiles: "Give me your tired, your poor, / Your huddled masses yearning to breathe free, / The wretched refuse of your teeming shore. / Send these, the homeless, tempest-tost to me, / I lift my lamp beside the golden door!" These hauntingly familiar phrases suggest on a fundamental level that the United States was built on a sense of diaspora and of welcoming exiles. Whether its borders will remain open to immigrants is a significant ethical issue for the citizens of the United States, and for Christians in the United States who hope to be other-oriented as Jesus commands. As monumental as these issues are, the immigrant paradigm does not account for the involuntary experience of the enslaved who were forced into being exiles. Clearly, U.S. history continues to be rife with conflicting stories about exile. My argument here enjoins Christians to be honest about those narratives as well as the new ones that have emerged since 9/11. Living diasporism might mean refusing to play out the entitled roles U.S. citizens are frequently cast in and rejecting the scripts that emphasize their being hurt and persecuted.

Such resistance more than likely encourages conflict as it is almost blasphemous or a sign of treason to speak in any other way after 9/11 than of being a victim. Especially in a context like New York City, and I would imagine in the nation's capital, hot spots where one must be really careful not to offend others by rehearsing anything other than what is acceptable to say about the traumatic events surrounding 9/11, Christians are chosen to relinquish the safe roles that they assume consciously or unconsciously. Put another way, in being about borders all of humanity and especially Christians are obligated to acknowledge and incarnate hybrid existence by embracing the leaky borders between the stories associated with the victim and those with the perpetrator.[50] Only then

---

[50] See Cynthia S. W. Crysdale, *Embracing Travail: Retrieving the Cross Today* (New York: Continuum, 1999), for a discussion of the need to understand and embrace ourselves not only as victims but also as aggressors and highlights the "fierce ambiguity" of living among these tensions within life (50).

can we become exiles, released from any emotional attachments to self, story, or place.

What I have tried to make plain throughout this book is that these are not just political claims, but even more than that they are theological convictions as well. Just as Jesus calls his followers to leave all their prized possessions behind, Christians are called to leave their emotional attachments to "the one true story" about suffering or injury after 9/11 behind and become emotional exiles. Christians are created and chosen to live with difference, to be hybrids in that there always is another story that pushes on them, that lives with them, although not always comfortably. Witnessing to the incarnation, whereby hybridity is sacralized, compels Christians further to live with difference, and the mystery and ambiguity that accompany it. Engaging otherness, and as a result relinquishing a privileged, singular self, place, or story—living as an emotional exile—is fundamental to living a Christian life.

Insisting on a diaspora existence, even an emotional and psychic one, treads on dangerous terrain. Author Philip Roth deals with an analogous type of perilous role traversing in his novel, *Operation Shylock*, in which the two main characters are named Philip Roth, one an imposter of the other.[51] The imposter uses the name of the author Philip Roth to gain influence and support for a new political program for Jewish people: Diasporism. For many Jews, identity is tied inextricably to the Holy Land; hence, such an idea seems preposterous, even profane. Not so for Roth's character double. For him, authentic Jewry means living in the diaspora by returning to one's European homeland. Diasporism is the only answer to Israel's failed mission, which has led to far too much violence and bloodshed—to the extent that Israel is giving Jews a bad name. In reinventing Shakespeare's Shylock from *The Merchant of Venice* against the backdrop of the Middle Eastern conflict, Roth implies that there is an even worse stereotype that is threatening Jewish existence with others: the militarist Israeli.[52] Since the oppressive tactics of the Israeli Defense Forces give the Jewish state a bad name, Roth abandons Zionist claims and embraces diasporism. Roth (the author and the character) is well aware of the danger of playing with images of Jewish identity, for one false move can essentialize Jewry indeterminately. His claims, albeit fictional, are so contentious that he creates an imposter to spread his

---

[51] Philip Roth, *Operation Shylock: A Confession* (New York: Simon & Schuster, 1993).
[52] Ibid., 274.

campaign. Although the Jew, or rather the stereotype of the Jew, has been on trial for hundreds of years, is it naïve to claim that Roth dares to play with this one stereotype, the Shylock, in hopes that others will realize the dangers of a posture of entitlement?

Much in the same way that being critical of the State of Israel after Auschwitz seems offensive, being about borders after 9/11 appears at the very least daring. In spite of this Christians in the United States are elected for a role reversal similar to Roth's. By retelling their stories about land and borders and hence exposing themselves and their fears to others, they can incarnate a being that is vigilant about borders by relinquishing and mourning any attachment to them in the first place. By rejecting the process of perpetually mourning the dead in order to secure one's claims to the land, Gopin refocuses the emotional impact of mourning in the Israeli-Palestinian crisis onto one's attachments: "The mourning would be over past exclusive ownership. This may not be able to take place for those who do not accept final boundaries, but for those who could, a powerful message would emerge."[53] In being about borders after 9/11, Christians analogously are chosen to mourn not only the dead but also any entitled feelings about place, modeling for others a type of existence that is based in charity.

Summary

I have argued that being about borders results in not only personal and religious implications but also political ones. Thinking through the stories about Israeli and Palestinian tensions, I propose that to be vigilant about borders almost always demands a scrutiny of the identities imposed on ourselves from outside and from within. Meeting someone in charity means being honest about the negative ways we are perceived and how an individual's or culture's actions may influence those perceptions. Some of us are so set on getting the story straight that we become blind to the feelings and perceptions of others. This is particularly evident around momentous and traumatic global events, such as the Shoah and 9/11. In being about borders, Christians need to reframe getting the story straight into a complex emotionally trying process in which one realizes that human existence cannot be limited to one true or pure story and

---

[53] Gopin, *Holy War, Holy Peace,* 205.

must capitulate to the cacophony of hybrid voices that are vying to be heard. In order to embrace the needs and feelings of the other, there must be less otherizing and naturalizing of borders between one another and more receptivity to the idea that because borders are indeed porous, the stories and character types of the people and cultures at them overlap and intertwine. Furthermore, there must be a commitment to being about borders to the extent that we relinquish any privilege associated with them, even the status of being a victim. In trying to imagine an existence based on emotionally letting go, on being an exile, on diaspora, Christians can begin to envision a life at the borders with Jesus.

Chapter 6

A Christian Anthropology of Difference

In hoping to advance a theological anthropology of difference, I have argued throughout this book that being vigilant about the emotional tenor of our relationships leads to the best practice at borders. While teachings about creation and the person and work of Christ certainly provide talking points on how difference and hybridity are part of the very essence of border life, we still may find ourselves asking: *How do I navigate through my everyday life in a world bursting with so many competing and overlapping stories? What should my commitment to emotional openness look like?* To answer these questions more explicit guidelines are needed. Psychological insights have the potential to further flesh out the challenges of our hybrid existence and emphasize the importance of being ready for and open to conflict, exposure, and mourning. Christians might even consider whether tactics employed in treating trauma can be used as a resource to help us think or, better yet, *feel* through the emotional dissonance of relating to one another in everyday life.

Clinical Approaches to Trauma

In contemporary treatment of trauma survivors, techniques are used to embrace the role that body and affect play in organizing one's life and relationships.[1] While in no way am I presuming that all of our interpersonal,

---

[1] Bessel A. van der Kolk is a leading clinician and researcher in this area; see van der Kolk "Beyond the Talking Cure: Somatic Experience and Subcortical Imprints in

interreligious, or international interactions with one another mirror the predicament of a person presenting with a complex history of trauma, I am curious whether techniques employed by clinicians in treating trauma survivors can help ordinary people become more vigilant about noticing how emotions impact their relationships. Engaging clinical and literary theories about trauma at this juncture is probably not surprising as many of the examples used in this book unfold in stories about trauma either explicitly or implicitly.

The clinical definition of trauma refers to the psychological cost a person pays after living through an event or series of events, such as chronic physical or sexual abuse, neglect, serious accidents, war, terrorism, natural disasters, or chronic or acute illness, which cannot be easily put into words. For the average person, "ordinary events generally are not relived as images, smells, physical sensations, or sounds associated with that event. Ordinarily, the remembered aspects of experience coalesce into a story that captures the essence of what has happened. As people remember and tell others about an event, the *narrative* gradually changes with time and telling."[2] Patients diagnosed with posttraumatic stress disorder (PTSD), however, are unable to integrate or contextualize the traumatic event into a coherent self-narrative; instead, the event remains fixed in the original moment. Victims of trauma experience the exact sounds, tastes, and feelings of the original event, probably because

---

the Treatment of Trauma," in *EMDR as an Integrative Psychotherapy Approach: Experts of Diverse Orientations Explore the Paradigm Prism*, ed. Francine Shapiro (Washington, DC: American Psychological Association Press, 2002), 57–83. Studies engaging trauma, particularly around the Shoah, 9/11, and even the recent tsunamis, have transcended the fields of psychiatry and psychology and are now part of the humanities. For work on trauma in literary theory, see Cathy Caruth, *Unclaimed Experience: Trauma, Narrative and History* (Baltimore, MD: Johns Hopkins University Press, 1996); and for a historical approach, I have already referred to Dominick LaCapra, *Writing History, Writing Trauma* (Baltimore, MD: Johns Hopkins University Press, 2001). More recently, the field of trauma studies has impacted scholars of pedagogy and writing composition; see Shane Borrowman, ed., *Trauma and the Teaching of Writing* (Albany: SUNY Press, 2005). It is noteworthy that theologians are beginning to engage trauma treatment and theory more explicitly in their work as well. See Serene Jones, *Trauma and Grace: Theology in a Ruptured World* (Louisville, KY: Westminster John Knox Press, 2009); and also Jennifer Erin Beste, *God and the Victim: Traumatic Intrusions on Grace and Freedom*, American Academy of Religion Series (Oxford: Oxford University Press, 2007).

[2] Bessel A. van der Kolk, "Posttraumatic Therapy in the Age of Neuroscience," *Psychoanalytic Dialogues* 12, no. 3 (2002): 382.

they are "too hyper- or hypo-aroused to be able to 'process' and communicate what they are experiencing. . . . The person may feel, see, or hear the sensory elements of the traumatic experience, but he or she may be psychologically prevented from being able to translate this experience into communicable language."[3] When reminded of the event, they return to it sensually and emotively and usually do not even know they are doing so. Symptoms of trauma include memories, senses, and feelings associated with the event intruding on other everyday experiences and activities in addition to the emergence of unregulated affect including extremes of rage, fear, and numbness. Trauma victims, like those burdened by narcissism, often avoid complicated emotional entanglements because such relations might trigger a posttraumatic response. As one might imagine, these symptoms can impact a person's development and social relations.

The most common treatment of trauma has focused on helping patients attach meaning to the event in question so they can gain perspective and control over it. This is the traditional psychoanalytic treatment or talking cure for trauma in which the analyst has the patient try to tell their story in hopes of exposing themselves to the source of their trauma so that they can eventually give it a context and integrate it into their identity, in other words, talk it into being. Such treatment privileges reason and discourse in that it is the patient's verbal connections that give the event meaning and context. Although analytic therapies may be useful in treating acute trauma—for example, someone who has been raped or witnessed a violent event—people with complex histories of trauma, including children who have been abused over long periods of time, may not be helped primarily with the talking cure because the trauma has interfered with communication within their brain, in some cases making telling a linear story impossible. In light of these challenges, in more and more clinical research it is being argued that body-based therapies that are attentive to irregularities in affect work better "to help survivors tolerate the sensory reminders of the trauma."[4] In cases of someone presenting with a history of complex trauma, giving the event a place in one's personal narrative may not effectively treat the other emotional irregularities triggered by their history. In being attentive to

---

[3] Bessel A. van der Kolk, "Posttraumatic Stress Disorder and the Nature of Trauma," in *Healing Trauma: Attachment, Mind, Body, and Brain*, ed. Marion F. Solomon and Daniel J. Siegel (New York: W.W. Norton & Co., 2003), 187.

[4] van der Kolk, "Posttraumatic Therapy," 381.

the response of the body to the event, as well as to the affective impact of the trauma experience, clinicians are able to help the patient regulate their emotions while also enhancing the quality of their interpersonal relations.

Although much of trauma treatment aims at having the patient understand the traumatic event and integrate it into his or her self story, the more important issue in contemporary research on trauma and for anyone working toward a corporeal theological anthropology is not pinpointing exactly what has happened letter-for-letter but rather being attentive to the emotional impact of the traumatic happening. In clinical settings, trauma victims sometimes tell contradictory and conflicting accounts of the event in question. Nonetheless, truth telling is not the main purpose of treatment. The truth of the traumatic event does not matter as much as the affective dissonance surrounding the event. Similarly, a theological anthropology of difference is not primarily concerned with the truth of border distinctions but instead considers if the affectively charged stories, memories, and feelings of all parties at the border have been attended to and embraced.

Goals of Trauma Treatment[5]

Clinicians generally set four goals for treating trauma patients, which I believe can be useful in developing a theological anthropology of difference. They include: creating a safe place for venting emotions, learning how to name emotions, paying attention to one's body, and opening to intimacy. Honing these skills enables the patient to respond to otherness in their everyday life and, even more relevant for our purposes, can lead those striving to be about borders to a type of human existence that engages conflict, exposure, and ultimately mourning.

Usually when one is faced with trauma all feelings of being safe and secure are lost. Trauma survivors may be reluctant to work through the traumatic event because that process entails dealing with the unregulated

---

[5] Referring to the work of van der Kolk, Marion F. Solomon broadly posits the following goals for treating trauma, including its effects on interpersonal relations; see Solomon, "Connection, Disruption, Repair: Treating the Effects of Attachment Trauma on Intimate Relationships," in *Healing Trauma*, 324. My husband, Ken Einhorn, who has worked with traumatized children and families at New York Foundling, helped me conceptualize these clinical goals more broadly so I could begin to integrate them into an anthropology of difference.

affect that accompanies the experience of the event, making the survivor feel unsafe all over again. Not surprisingly, one of the first therapeutic goals for people suffering from trauma is to create a safe environment in which intense emotions can unfold and be maintained, to provide an outlet for the unregulated affect, the sadness, rage, grief, and shame, that often accompanies trauma reactions. Analogously, when an ordinary person encounters difference, whether on a one-to-one basis or on a communal level, unexpected emotion or unregulated affect emerges. Whether the circumstance is related to family systems and parenting, interreligious relationships and the ongoing dialogue between Jews and Catholics, or the international conflict between the Israelis and the Palestinians or between the United States and its ambiguous enemies, we have seen that the interruptive feelings that surface in daily encounters are not easily negotiated. Such feelings have a history and are typically connected to old hurts, making locating a safe place for them to be expressed either privately or publicly necessary yet difficult.

In transitioning from a clinical situation to everyday life, we must designate places that can serve as safe environments to express our unruly emotions to one another. These sanctuaries need to allow all frustrations to be heard yet not necessarily reconciled. Families could set a time for venting frustrations with the assurance that anything expressed would *not* be used against anyone either at that point or at a later time. Within the larger community, parishes, synagogues, or other institutions, such as schools, hospitals, and social service organizations, could hold workshops in which one would feel free to discuss the institutional issues that create affective disturbances. In such a safe place conflicting feelings related to religious intolerance, racism, sexism, or even homophobia might be addressed.[6]

While power inequities may complicate and compromise these local initiatives for creating safe settings for dealing with affective dissonance, probably most challenging is building safe venues within the global arena and the world of politics because of the constant surveillance of the media. In the public eye, there is less room for genuinely engaging extreme emotions. Any show of intense affect within the realm of politics

---

[6] For a discussion of the need to create forums in ecclesial settings to address "taboo topics," see Bradford E. Hinze, *Practices of Dialogue in the Roman Catholic Church: Aims and Obstacles, Lessons and Laments* (New York: Continuum, 2006), 246–48. Moreover, for more on the spirituality of creating safe spaces, see Teresa Rhodes McGee, *Transforming Trauma: A Path toward Wholeness* (Maryknoll, NY: Orbis Books, 2005), 126–27.

or celebrity is used to sell more papers and buy more airtime, in other words, is sensationalized and exploited for economic and political gain. It appears that it is more socially acceptable to hide one's anger than to show it. What's more, any resistance to the façade of gentility and any full-out capitulation to rage are categorized as primitive and uncivilized. The pervasive view of thinking about peace in terms of a simple handshake and affect as a sign of unreasonable rage needs to be altered for being about borders to emerge within the global landscape. As already discussed, there are affectively charged moments that the public can swallow easily, for instance, those intense moments of outpouring of grief over the dead and injured after 9/11. Nonetheless, for healing to occur within the global landscape, the public needs to be able to stomach other displays of feelings as well. In other words, a venue needs to be created for airing affective dissonance in the public realm, one that is viewed not as a sensationalist talk show but as a safe haven for everyone's emotions, even the disturbing and unexpected ones. For this to occur, media analysis would need to expand in depth so that the public's gaze would be supported and challenged by more than sound bite coverage. Moreover, in addition to having political, economic, and religious commentary by experts in the field, it might help to have psychological commentary on world events in order to assist the viewer in understanding how emotion shapes one another's stories, feelings, and memories about oneself, the other, and all the spaces in-between.

After revealing one's feelings in a safe environment, another goal in affect-oriented trauma treatment is to name these feelings in order to gain perspective on them. Naming them, or "labeling" them as often expressed in psychological discourse, creates a reality for what was previously unsayable or what was kept under the table. It calls one's feelings into being and demands that they are acknowledged by one another. For trauma survivors, naming emotions is difficult because it requires a distance from the traumatic event at the same time it asks one to become intellectually comfortable with the event. When encountering difference, the stakes are certainly not as high as with someone struggling with a complex history of trauma, yet the act of naming feelings is still risky. When I name that I am angry or sad I am revealing that I need more than I am getting, and in the process I am exposing myself to the other with no real grasp of how that act of exposure will be received. Will they lash out at me? Will they run away? Perhaps, even worse, will they not hear my feelings at all?

This practice of naming emotions would unfold uniquely for each of the situations covered in this book. We might have to be open to discussing publicly why there seems to be only one acceptable script when speaking about motherhood, specifically that of the good mother who should feel lucky she has children. Also in relation to parenting, in a family meeting, the emotions festering beneath the heated issues would need to be articulated, in which a son might say, "I am feeling angry because of x." Between religious groups, one group might name what they are feeling as frustration of not being heard in regard to a specific issue. In the context of world relations, this again becomes arguably more difficult. Still, Christians could discuss these international issues and name their feelings in small groups in ecclesial settings. In each scenario, labeling one's feelings integrates our affective and cognitive processes, creating the potential for life-giving, corporeal dialogue. Naming deals head-on with the problem of the *differend* in which parties cannot express the meaning of the crisis at the border. In naming emotions, priority is given to feeling rather than to thought, leading each party to expose one's vulnerability in an effort to hear and be heard.

Feelings, however, cannot be properly identified and named without paying rigorous attention to one's embodied experiences. A concurrent goal to naming emotions, then, is being attuned to how affect is building in one's body before it becomes debilitating. This requires being vigilant about changes in one's body's responses to border situations, such as a tightening in one's throat or profuse perspiration. In addition to promoting a dialogue that is more body-conscious, becoming aware of the connection between body and emotion empowers the person to have more control of their situation, preventing them from easily falling into the same emotional patterns.[7] When a person or group publicly processes or explains the physiological changes occurring within their body to the other who has never recognized it, the limits of discursive dialogue might become evident to everyone involved, and feelings become more easily identifiable. Avoiding the pain of the other at your table is easier when you have only heard about it; nevertheless, when the physical manifestations of it become readily apparent, evading it seems irresponsible, unjust, and uncharitable. For being about borders to take shape in any of the situations addressed in this book, we would need to hear more

---

[7] For more on the importance of being attentive to body processes in treatment sessions, see van der Kolk, "Posttraumatic Therapy," 389.

about one another's bodily reactions to the process of parenting, ethnic conflicts, ecclesial developments, and geopolitical happenings. When we witness to one another's suffering in an embodied way, it reveals human vulnerability and arguably makes it far less easy to dehumanize others since it becomes obvious that they have bodily limits similar to our own.

A final goal is to grapple with the fear of intimacy with others in relationships, since for clinicians this is the root of our inability to deal with the emotions of others. This gets to the heart of the narcissistic tendencies in all of us discussed in the first chapter and demands asking the difficult questions of why we are petrified of appearing vulnerable to others. This would take some honest talk in both interpersonal and communal contexts. In our interpersonal interactions with one another this might mean that parents would have to admit that they need their children as much as their children need them and own up to how that need scares them to the point of feeling like they are out of control. Regarding the emotional tumult over the canonization of Edith Stein, dealing with a fear of intimacy might mean that both parties, Catholics and Jews, would have to admit how their sacred stories are enmeshed with one another. It might also require reflection on whether it is helpful or hurtful to a relationship to hold on to the idea that one person or group has suffered more than another. Building intimacy in this situation would involve both parties relinquishing any attachment to being a victim as that identity often prevents people from embracing the connections between one another. On the international level, this would involve letting go of any closed entitled stance at the borders, even to the point of relinquishing one's place at the borders all together. Embodying a type of diaspora existence on the individual or communal level in which one's self, story, and place is always, already connected and enmeshed with another is the heart of what it means to overcome fears of intimacy and to embrace the chaotic affective implications of one's proximity with another.

In sum, whether treating someone who has experienced trauma or in dealing with troubled relationships with those who are different at the border, it is necessary to construct the right setting for healing to occur. It is not enough to welcome disparate negative emotions; more than that, they need to be named and reflected upon in a safe context. As Christians attempt to be about borders in their own life, meaning being human in a way that acknowledges, respects, and manages difference, these same techniques may be employed in dealing with affective responses to otherness. By creating safe places for encounter to unfold, becoming adept at naming their emotions and those of others, becoming more aware of the role that body language plays in border encounters, and actively working toward building intimacy, Christians can begin to live out an anthropology of difference.

Rules of Engagement

Beyond the test cases I pose throughout the book, it is up to all of us to imagine what being about borders in our own lives might look like. Each of us has our own borders with which we must contend. I confront the emotional fallout from borders in my marriage, with my children, among my extended family, with my students, among my colleagues, and within the academy. Whatever the border situation, there are some basic rules of engagement in a Christian anthropology of difference, which illuminates the centrality of affect in our lives. By sticking to these five rules in our border engagements, Christians can perhaps more genuinely honor the call to incarnate hybrid existence—a way of being human that is respectful of theological accounts of creation and the person and work of Christ.

Rule #1: Pay Attention to Affect

Just plain not feeling right or detecting "affective disturbances" is the first and most important clue that one has encountered a border of some sort. We may be engaging with a friend or colleague on one or another issue and sense intuitively that something about the interaction feels off. Perhaps the other retreats from the engagement. Or perhaps, this strange interaction represents an elongated time period of not "clicking" with the other person.

Detecting such discontinuities is easier in some situations than others. In this day and age of ever-proliferating communication technology, including e-mail, text messaging, and even blogging, we may be enabled to become blind to or ignorant of affective disturbances. Even those media have their own grammars and rhythm, however, and one can still feel emotionally off in relation to another. At times, deeper reflection is needed to discern whether one is overreacting to the situation or if indeed one has broached a border of some kind.

To be sure, feeling something unexpected in our ordinary dealings with one another provides us with the opportunity to ignore, run from, or be about borders. At such an emotional crossroad, our inclination may be to directly ask the other if something is wrong and if they have been hurt or offended in some way, but more often than not, this direct confrontation is premature. Before dealing with the conflict and exposing one's feelings, one might need to create a setting in which everyone feels safe.

Rule #2: Make Everyone Feel Comfortable

If in our inclination to be about borders it does not seem wise to address the situation head on with words, a better strategy might be to make room for the other emotionally, and this includes listening to the other as they attempt to communicate their stories. Communication is not just a matter of words; it encompasses unexpected body language, gesture, disparities in affect, rhythm, and even moments of silence. Accordingly, all parties have a responsibility not only to heed one's stories through linguistic discourse, but through one another's gestures, tone, and so on. Successful trauma treatment teaches us that people feel comfortable being open to the difficult emotions of relating to others when they feel safe, and such safety is created by allowing for the other to emote without interruption or judgment. It means inviting someone into your world without a prescribed script for conversation. One needs to create a place where one feels comfortable to be uncomfortable emotionally.

Creating a safe emotional environment might seem contradictory or at least counterintuitive to my previous comments about how in an effort to be about borders each one of us is called to emotional homelessness or diaspora existence. Doesn't the notion "diaspora" connote a lack of home, and hence a lack of security? In using trauma treatment to think through what it means to be about borders in the midst of hybrid existence, one must start to allow for another's affect to have priority over one's own. Taking leave of one's own emotional security can ensure, or at the very least create the possibility for, the other's emotional safety. Sometimes we have to resist feeling comfortable at the expense of another. We have to, employing the words of LaCapra, seek "empathic ensettlement" in our lives. This should not be read as negative or depressing, since being about borders is not a matter of *always* feeling uncomfortable; rather, it is the process that accounts for and pauses at moments in which things feel off, ultimately striving to figure out why that is the case. In an effort to make everyone feel emotionally safe, one needs to ask the difficult emotional questions. Are someone's needs, feelings, memories, and stories being ignored by mine? Are my needs, feelings, memories, and stories being obscured by those of another? Feeling uncomfortable allows us to attend to the sin of *scotoma*—of being blind to the existence of another and their feeling—all in an effort to make them feel safe.

Rule #3: Employ Storytelling as a Type of Praxis

Once people feel safe, it may be the right moment to take the next step of revealing our hybrid identities—of telling our stories that overlap and intertwine with another even if we wish they did not. Storytelling, as we have seen, is a complex process of negotiating fact from fiction and, most important, privileging all the emotions of the in-between. Those feelings are symbolic of profound needs, wants, and desires. Utilizing trauma treatment here, once a safe place is created, one needs to develop skills at becoming aware of their emotions through labeling them. It is not enough to be angry over something that happened in the past; one needs to say, "I am angry." Then one needs to say, "I am angry because of *x*." They need to reveal their stories—the spatial trajectories that inform their reality. Exposing oneself in such a way invites others to enter into an unpredictable, operatic, and genuine relationship in which everyone's needs, feelings, memories, and stories are engaged.

It helps if there is decorum throughout the praxis of storytelling. Listening and silently making cognitive and affective connections with memories and events from that of another are just as important and necessary as doing the talking. Conflict and exposure happen both ways, in putting your stories out there for the other to engage and revising your own stories when you hear the needs, feelings, memories, and stories of another. This is the point when the contentious emotions around memory occur; this is when we are called to re-member in a way that honors the existence of the other whom we meet at the border.

Re-membering has the potential to foster intimacy, creating the opportunity to embrace one another as multistoried selves, some stories of which are enmeshed with others. The work of memory calls us to rewrite our own stories in relation to that of another. Consequently, in hearing the other we may need to revise our stories, relinquishing the privilege of the "one true story." Such relinquishment is painful as it points to a

loss, which must be grieved so one can be transformed and even converted to incarnating hybrid existence. Surrendering the one pure, true
story about any single privileged identity and mourning it moves us
from a position of sin to a state of grace. It is the start of healing and the
hope for future reconciliation and peace in a world of others.

Rule #4: Keep Watch for Others

One should always be vigilant about the arrival of another—this could
be another story, another person, or even another group. Growing up in
an Italian American family it was customary to think that one could
never have enough food for a celebration. There were all sorts of reasons
for this sentiment, and one of them was that one never could be sure
how many people might show up for the party. This overabundance of
food and drink is Italian American hospitality at its best. Nevertheless,
what I am alluding to here is more than having enough to eat; it is also
having a plan for physically making more room for another at the table
and, even more important, for allowing the new arrivals emotional space
to share their stories. In being about borders, one needs to be open to
the notion that human existence is always changing and evolving; it is
unfinished business. Accepting this creates a context for answering the
call to live in the image of God and to honor the incarnation in that we
accept our human limits and our vulnerability as a sacred sign of the
presence of another.

Rule #5: Know When to Retreat and Be Sure to Return

When the emotional tenor of the border encounter becomes too hot,
many of us want to run for the hills. This is not always cowardly. In some
ways, it could be respectful of our own needs and those of another in
that at some point in our lives many of us have experienced either need-
ing space or being asked to give another space. What we usually mean
by "space" is emotional distance, and space in this context might mean
retreating from the border situation because it is too painful. In most
cases, this cannot and should not be the end to the story or, better yet,
to the relationship. While we might need to take leave of the border to
protect our emotional selves, we should return to it, continuing the work
of vigilance. Knowing when to leave and when to return represent difficult decisions, requiring emotional work and sophistication that pays

attention to the clues in affect in order to build and maintain right relationships in a world with others.

Such emotional work and sophistication is not natural for us, and, not surprisingly, there are no easy ways to enact any of these rules of engagement. In many ways we are chosen for extremely perilous work—to feel our way about treacherous borders, sites plagued by disorienting blind spots and uncomfortable emotional chasms. Our only option is to remain vigilant. We have seen the devastation from human neglect of borders, the harm done to individuals, groups, and even nations. The Christian anthropology of difference being presented here responds to our neglect and calls for a life of emotional awareness of the other to the point of being "undone." Butler explains: "To be undone by another is a primary necessity, an anguish, to be sure, but also a chance—to be addressed, be claimed, bound to what is not me, but also to be moved, to be prompted to act, to address myself elsewhere, and so to vacate the self-sufficient 'I' as a kind of possession."[8] Such a way of being human bears witness to the unpredictable and uncontrollable affective otherness that borders bring. The open-ended component to being about borders subverts the tendency to expect certain rewards in interpersonal, interreligious, and international relations, prophetically calling for a way of being human oriented toward the unknown, for the things not hoped for.

[8] Judith Butler, *Giving an Account of Oneself* (New York: Fordham University Press, 2005), 136.

Bibliography

Anderson, Victor. *Beyond Ontological Blackness: An Essay on African American Religious and Cultural Criticism*. New York: Continuum, 1995.

Anzaldúa, Gloria. *Borderlands/La Frontera: The New Mestiza*. San Francisco: Aunt Lute Books, 1987.

Ariel, David S. *What Do Jews Believe? The Spiritual Foundations of Judaism*. New York: Schocken Books, 1995.

Balsamo, Anne. *Technologies of the Body: Reading Cyborg Women*. Durham: Duke University Press, 1996.

Bammer, Angelika. "The Dilemma of the 'But': Writing Germanness After the Holocaust." In *Borders, Exiles, Diasporas*, edited by Elazar Barkan and Marie-Denise Shelton, 15–31. Stanford: Stanford University Press, 1998.

Barger, Lilian Calles. *Eve's Revenge: Women and a Spirituality of the Body*. Grand Rapids, MI: Brazos Press, 2003.

Bartel, Michelle J. *What It Means to Be Human: Living with Others before God*. Louisville, KY: Geneva Press, 2001.

Beattie, Tina. *God's Mother, Eve's Advocate: A Marian Narrative of Women's Salvation*. London: Continuum, 2002.

Beste, Jennifer Erin. *God and the Victim: Traumatic Intrusions on Grace and Freedom*. American Academy of Religion Series. Oxford: Oxford University Press, 2007.

Bhabha, Homi, K. *The Location of Culture*. London: Routledge, 1994.

Borowitz, Eugene B. *Renewing the Covenant: A Theology for the Postmodern Jew*. Philadelphia: The Jewish Publication Society, 1991.

Borrowman, Shane, ed. *Trauma and the Teaching of Writing*. Albany: SUNY Press, 2005.

Boyarin, Daniel, and Jonathan Boyarin. *Powers of Diaspora: Two Essays on the Relevance of Jewish Culture*. Minneapolis: University of Minnesota Press, 2002.

Butler, Judith. *Giving an Account of Oneself*. New York: Fordham University Press, 2005.

———. *Precarious Life: The Powers of Mourning and Violence*. London: Verso, 2004.

Carroll, James. *Constantine's Sword: The Church and the Jews*. New York: Houghton Mifflin Company, 2001.

Caruth, Cathy. *Unclaimed Experience: Trauma, Narrative and History*. Baltimore, MD: Johns Hopkins University Press, 1996.

Cavanaugh, William T. "Migrant, Tourist, Pilgrim, Monk: Mobility and Identity in a Global Age." *Theological Studies* 69, no. 2 (2008): 340–56.

The Charter of Allah: The Platform of the Islamic Resistance Movement (Hamas), 1988. http://www.palestinecenter.org/cpap/documents/charter.html (accessed October 7, 2007).

Coles, Robert. *The Call of Stories: Teaching and the Moral Imagination*. Boston: Houghton Mifflin Company, 1989.

Commission for Religious Relations with the Jews. We Remember: A Reflection on the Shoah, March 16, 1998. http://www.vatican.va/roman_curia /pontifical_councils/chrstuni/documents/rc_pc_chrstuni_doc_16031998 _shoah_en.html (accessed September 5, 2007).

Committee on Doctrine and Committee on Ecumenical and Interreligious Affairs, USCCB. "A Note on Ambiguities Contained in 'Reflections on Covenant and Mission,'" June 18, 2009. http://www.ccjr.us/dialogika-resources /documents-and-statements/roman-catholic/us-conference-of-catholic -bishops/578-usccb-09june18 (accessed June 30, 2010).

The Congregation for the Doctrine of the Faith. On the Unicity and Salvific Universality of Jesus Christ and the Church (*Dominus Iesus*), August 6, 2000. http://www.vatican.va/roman_curia/congregations/cfaith/documents /rc_con_cfaith_doc_20000806_dominus-iesus_en.html (accessed September 5, 2007).

Coonan, Terry, and Robin Thompson. "Ancient Evil, Modern Face: The Fight Against Human Trafficking." *Georgetown Journal of International Affairs* 6, no. 1 (January 1, 2005): 43–51. http://www.library.manhattan.edu:2612/ (accessed August 24, 2010).

Copeland, M. Shawn. *Enfleshing Freedom: Body, Race, and Being*. Minneapolis: Fortress Press, 2010.

Crisp, Oliver. *Divinity and Humanity: The Incarnation Reconsidered*. Cambridge, UK: Cambridge University Press, 2007.

Crysdale, Cynthia S. W. *Embracing Travail: Retrieving the Cross Today*. New York: Continuum, 1999.

Damasio, Antonio. *The Feeling of What Happens: Body and Emotion in the Making of Consciousness*. New York: Harcourt Brace & Company, 1999.

de Certeau, Michel. *The Practice of Everyday Life*. Translated by Steven Rendall. Berkeley: University of California Press, 1984.

Diagnostic and Statistical Manual of Mental Disorders (DSM-IV-TR). 4th ed. text rev. Arlington, VA: American Psychiatric Association, 2000.

Doran, Robert M. *Subject and Psyche*. 2nd ed. Milwaukee, WI: Marquette University Press, 1994.

Driscoll, Craig. *Of the Cross: The Life of Blessed Edith Stein*. Manila, Philippines: Sinag-Tala Publishers, 1987.

Dulles, Avery. "Covenant and Mission." *America: The National Catholic Weekly* 187, no. 12 (October 21, 2002). http://www.americamagazine.org/content /article.cfm?article_id=2550 (accessed September 5, 2007).

Ehrensaft, Diane. *Spoiling Childhood: How Well-Meaning Parents Are Giving Children Too Much—But Not What They Need*. New York: The Guilford Press, 1997.

Eidelson, Judy I., and Roy J. Eidelson. "Dangerous Ideas: Five Beliefs that Propel Groups toward Conflict." *American Psychologist* 58, no. 3 (2003): 182–92.

Ellis, Marc H. *O, Jerusalem! The Contested Future of the Jewish Covenant*. Minneapolis: Fortress Press, 1999.

Finkelstein, Norman G. *Image and Reality of the Israel-Palestine Conflict*. 2nd rev. ed. London: Verso, 2003.

Flannery, Austin, ed. *Vatican Council II: Constitutions, Decrees, Declarations*. Northport, NY: Costello Publishing Co., 1996.

Freud, Sigmund. "Mourning and Melancholia." In *The Standard Edition of the Complete Psychological Works of Sigmund Freud*, translated by James Strachey. Vol. 14, 243–58. London: The Hogarth Press, 1957.

Friedman, Thomas L. *From Beirut to Jerusalem*. Updated with a New Chapter. New York: Random House, 1995.

Godzieba, Anthony J. "Incarnation, Theory, and Catholic Bodies: What Should Post-Postmodern Catholic Theology Look Like?" *Louvain Studies* 28 (2003): 217–31.

Goizueta, Roberto S. *Caminemos con Jesús: Toward a Hispanic/Latino Theology of Accompaniment*. Maryknoll, NY: Orbis Books, 1995.

———. " 'There You Will See Him': Christianity Beyond the Frontier Myth." In *The Church as Counterculture*, edited by Michael L. Budde and Robert W. Brimlow, 171–93. Albany: SUNY Press, 2000.

Gopin, Marc. *Holy War, Holy Peace: How Religion Can Bring Peace to the Middle East*. New York: Oxford University Press, 2002.

Greenstein, Ran. *Genealogies of Conflict: Class, Identity, and State in Palestine/Israel and South Africa*. Hanover, NH: University Press of New England, 1995.

Grosbard, Ofer. *Israel on the Couch: The Psychology of the Peace Process*. Albany: SUNY Press, 2003.

Haraway, Donna. *Simians, Cyborgs, and Women: The Reinvention of Nature*. New York: Routledge, 1991.

Hardt, Michael, and Antonio Negri. *Empire*. Cambridge, MA: Harvard University Press, 2000.

Herbstrith, Waltraud. *Edith Stein: A Biography*. Translated by Bernard Bonowitz. 2nd Eng. ed. San Francisco: Ignatius Press, 1992.

———, ed. *Never Forget: Christian and Jewish Perspectives on Edith Stein*. Translated by Susanne Batzdorff. Washington, DC: ICS Publications/Institute of Carmelite Studies, 1998.

Hermans, Hubert J. M., and Harry J.G. Kempen. "Moving Cultures: The Perilous Problems of Cultural Dichotomies in a Globalizing Society." *American Psychologist* 53, no. 10 (1998): 1111–20.

Hewitt, Kim. *Mutilating the Body: Identity in Blood and Ink*. Bowling Green, OH: Bowling Green State University Popular Press, 1997.

Hill Fletcher, Jeannine. *Monopoly on Salvation? A Feminist Approach to Religious Pluralism*. New York: Continuum, 2005.

Hinze, Bradford E. *Practices of Dialogue in the Roman Catholic Church: Aims and Obstacles, Lessons and Laments*. New York: Continuum, 2006.

———. "When Dialogue Leads to the Reform of Tradition." In *Tradition and Tradition Theories: An International Discussion*, edited by Thorsten Larbig and Siegfried Wiedenhofer, 336–55. Münster: Lit Verlag, 2006.

John Paul II. Address of His Holiness John Paul II for the 25th Anniversary Celebration of the Declaration "*Nostra Aetate*," December 6, 1990. http://www.vatican.va/holy_father/john_paul_ii/speeches/1990/december/documents/hf_jp-ii_spe_19901206_xxv-nostra-aetate-en.html (accessed September 5, 2007).

————. On the Permanent Validity of the Church's Missionary Mandate (*Redemptoris Missio*), December 7, 1990. http://www.vatican.va/holy_father/john_paul_ii/encyclicals/documents/hf_jp-ii_enc_07121990_redemptoris-missio_en.html (accessed September 5, 2007).

Johnson, Elizabeth A. *Quest for the Living God: Mapping Frontiers in the Theology of God*. New York: Continuum, 2007.

Jones, Serene. *Feminist Theory and Christian Theology: Cartographies of Grace*. Minneapolis: Fortress Press, 2000.

————. *Trauma and Grace: Theology in a Ruptured World*. Louisville, KY: Westminster John Knox Press, 2009.

Jones, Serene, and Paul Lakeland, eds. *Constructive Theology: A Contemporary Approach to Classical Themes*. Minneapolis: Fortress Press, 2005.

Kaplan, Mordecai M. *The Future of the American Jew*. New York: Reconstructionist Press, 1967.

————. *Judaism as a Civilization: Toward a Reconstruction of American-Jewish Life*. New York: Schocken Books, 1967.

————. *The Religion of Ethical Nationhood: Judaism's Contribution to World Peace*. London: The Macmillan Company, 1970.

Kawash, Samira. *Dislocating the Color Line: Identity, Hybridity, and Singularity in African-American Narrative*. Stanford, CA: Stanford University Press, 1997.

Kellner, Menachem. "Chosenness, Not Chauvinsm: Maimonides on the Chosen People." In *A People Apart: Chosenness and Ritual in Jewish Philosophical Thought*, edited by Daniel H. Frank, 51–75. Albany: SUNY Press, 1993.

Khan, Arshad. *Islam, Muslims, and America: Understanding the Basis of Their Conflict*. New York: Algora Publishing, 2003.

Kleinfield, N. R. "As 9/11 Nears, a Debate Rises: How Much Tribute Is Enough?" *New York Times*, September 2, 2007. 1. *Academic Search Premier, EBSCOhost* (accessed August 24, 2010).

Kline, Christina Baker, ed. *Child of Mine: Writers Talk about the First Year of Motherhood*. New York: Hyperion, 1997.

Kohut, Heinz. *The Analysis of the Self: A Systematic Approach to the Psychoanalytic Treatment of Narcissistic Personality Disorders*. New York: International Universities Press, Inc., 1971.

————. *The Restoration of Self*. Madison, WI: International Universities Press, Inc., 1977.

Kristeva, Julia. "Motherhood According to Giovanni Bellini." Chap. 9 (pp. 237–70) in *Desire in Language: A Semiotic Approach to Literature and Art*, edited by Leon S. Roudiez, translated by Thomas Gora, Alice Jardine, and Leon S. Roudiez. New York: Columbia University Press, 1980.

———. "Stabat Mater." In *Tales of Love*, translated by Leon S. Roudiez, 234–63. New York: Columbia University Press, 1987.

Kwok Pui-lan. *Postcolonial Imagination and Feminist Theology*. Louisville, KY: Westminster John Knox Press, 2005.

LaCapra, Dominick. *Writing History, Writing Trauma*. Baltimore, MD: Johns Hopkins University Press, 2001.

La Guardia, Anton. *War Without End: Israelis, Palestinians, and the Struggle for a Promised Land*. New York: St. Martin's Press, 2001.

Lasch, Christopher. *The Culture of Narcissism: American Life in an Age of Diminishing Expectations*. New York: W.W. Norton & Company, Inc., 1979.

———. *The Minimal Self: Psychic Survival in Troubled Times*. New York: W.W. Norton & Company, 1984.

LeDoux, Joseph. "The Self: Clues from the Brain." *Annals of New York Academy of Sciences* 1001 (2003): 295–304.

Levinas, Emmanuel. *Alterity and Transcendence*. Translated by Michael B. Smith. New York: Columbia University Press, 1999.

———. *Otherwise than Being or Beyond Essence*. Translated by Alphonso Lingis. Pittsburgh: Duquesne University Press, 1998.

Lonergan, Bernard J. F. *Collected Works of Bernard Lonergan*. Edited by Frederick E. Crowe and Robert Doran. Vol. 3, *Insight: A Study of Human Understanding*. Toronto: University of Toronto Press, 1997.

———. *Method in Theology*. Toronto: University of Toronto Press, 1990.

Lowen, Alexander. *Narcissism: Denial of the True Self*. New York: Macmillan Publishing Co., 1983.

Lyotard, Jean François. *The Differend: Phrases in Dispute*. Translated by Georges Van Den Abbeele. Minneapolis: University of Minnesota Press, 1988.

Mazzoni, Cristina. *Maternal Impressions: Pregnancy and Childbirth in Literature and Theory*. Ithaca, NY: Cornell University Press, 2002.

McGaugh, James. *Learning and Memory: An Introduction*. San Francisco: Albion Pub. Co., 1973.

McGowan, Daniel, and Marc H. Ellis, eds. *Remembering Deir Yassin: The Future of Israel and Palestine*. Brooklyn: Olive Branch Press, 1998.

Mendel, Gregor. *Experiments in Plant-Hybridisation*. Cambridge, MA: Harvard University Press, 1938; orig. 1866.

Miller-McLemore, Bonnie J. *Also a Mother: Work and Family as Theological Dilemma*. Nashville, TN: Abingdon Press, 1994.

Moser, Bob. "The Murder of a Boy Named GWEN." *Rolling Stone* 968 (February 24, 2005): 60–65. *Academic Search Premier*, EBSCO*host* (accessed August 24, 2010).

The National Council of Synagogues and The Bishops Committee for Ecumenical and Interreligious Affairs, USCCB. Reflections on Covenant and Mission, August 12, 2002. http://www.bc.edu/research/cjl/meta-elements/texts/cjrelations/resources/documents/interreligious/ncs_usccb120802.htm (accessed September 5, 2007).

The New Oxford Annotated Bible with the Apocrypha. New Revised Standard Version. Edited by Bruce M. Metzger and Roland E. Murphy. New York: Oxford University Press, 1994.

Obama, Barack. "Sen. Barack Obama Addresses Race at the Constitution Center in Philadelphia" *Washington Post*, March 18, 2008. http://www.washingtonpost.com/wp-dyn/content/article/2008/03/18/AR2008031801081.html (accessed March 21, 2008).

O'Brien, Tim. "How to Tell a True War Story." In *The Things They Carried*, 75–91. Boston: Houghton Mifflin, 1990.

Ovid. *Metamorphoses*. Translated by Rolfe Humphries. Bloomington: Indiana University Press, 1983.

Paulsell, Stephanie. *Honoring the Body: Meditations on a Christian Practice*. San Francisco: Jossey-Bass, 2002.

Perry, Joshua E., Larry R. Churchill, and Howard S. Kirshner. "The Terri Schiavo Case: Legal, Ethical, and Medical Perspectives." *Annals of Internal Medicine* 143, no. 10 (November 15, 2005): 744–48. http://www.library.manhattan.edu:2612/ (accessed August 24, 2010).

Plaskow, Judith. "Woman as Body: Motherhood and Dualism." *Anima* 8, no. 1 (Fall 1981): 56–67.

Plaut, W. Gunther. *The Case for the Chosen People*. Garden City, NY: Doubleday & Company, Inc., 1965.

The Qur'an. Translated by Abdullah Yusaf Ali. Elmhurst, NY: Tahrike Tarsile Qur'an, Inc., 2006.

Radford Ruether, Rosemary, and Herman J. Ruether. *The Wrath of Jonah: The Crisis of Religious Nationalism in the Israeli-Palestinian Conflict*. 2nd ed. Minneapolis: Fortress Press, 2002.

Rhodes McGee, Teresa. *Transforming Trauma: A Path toward Wholeness*. Maryknoll, NY: Orbis Books, 2005.

Rich, Adrienne. *Of Woman Born: Motherhood as Experience and Institution*. New York: Bantam Books, 1976.

Ricoeur, Paul. *Memory, History, Forgetting*. Translated by Kathleen Blamey and David Pellauer. Chicago: University of Chicago Press, 2004.

Roth, Philip. *Operation Shylock: A Confession*. New York: Simon & Schuster, 1993.

Ruddick, Sara. *Maternal Thinking: Toward a Politics of Peace*. Boston: Beacon Press, 1989.

Said, Edward W. "Reflections on Exile." Chap. 17 (pp. 173–86) in *Reflections on Exile and Other Essays*. Cambridge, MA: Harvard University Press, 2000.

Samuelson, Robert J. *The Good Life and Its Discontents: The American Dream in the Age of Entitlement 1945–1995*. New York: Times Books/Random House, 1995.

Scharer, Matthias, and Bernd Jochen Hilberath. *The Practice of Communicative Theology: Introduction to a New Theological Culture*. New York: Crossroad Publishing Co., 2008.

Setzer, Claudia. "Three Odd Couples: Women and Men in Mark and John." In *Mariam, the Magdalen, and the Mother*, edited by Deirdre Good, 75–92. Bloomington: Indiana University Press, 2005.

Shildrick, Margrit. *Leaky Bodies and Boundaries: Feminism, Postmodernism, and (Bio) ethics*. London: Routledge, 1997.

Slonimsky, Henry. Introduction to *The Kuzari: An Argument for the Faith of Israel*, by Judah Halevi. New York: Schocken Books, 1964.

Solomon, Marion F., and Daniel J. Siegel, eds. *Healing Trauma: Attachment, Mind, Body, and Brain*. New York: W.W. Norton & Co., 2003.

Spoto, Donald. *Reluctant Saint: The Life of Francis of Assisi*. New York: Viking Compass, 2002.

Stein, Edith. *Essays on Woman: The Collected Works of Edith Stein*. Vol. 2. Edited by L. Gelber and Romaeus Leuven. Translated by Freda Mary Oben. 2nd rev. ed. Washington, DC: ICS Publications, 1996.

———. *Life in a Jewish Family: The Collected Works of Edith Stein*. Vol. 1. Edited by L. Gelber and Romaeus Leuven. Translated by Josephine Koeppel. Washington, DC: ICS Publications, 1986.

————. *On the Problem of Empathy: The Collected Works of Edith Stein*. Vol. 3. Translated by Waltraut Stein. 3rd rev. ed. Washington, DC: ICS Publications, 1989.

————. *Science of the Cross: The Collected Works of Edith Stein*. Vol. 6. Edited by L. Gelber and Romaeus Leuven. Translated by Josephine Koeppel. Washington, DC: ICS Publications, 1998.

Tannen, Deborah. *That's Not What I Meant: How Conversation Style Makes or Breaks Relationships*. New York: Ballantine Books, 1986.

Taylor, Charles. "Kant's Theory of Freedom." Chap. 12 (pp. 318–37) in *Philosophical Papers: Volume 2, Philosophy and the Human Sciences*. Cambridge, UK: Cambridge University Press, 1985.

Vacek, Edward Collins. *Love, Human and Divine: The Heart of Christian Ethics*. Washington, DC: Georgetown University Press, 1994.

van der Kolk, Bessel A. "Beyond the Talking Cure: Somatic Experience and Subcortical Imprints in the Treatment of Trauma." In *EMDR as an Integrative Psychotherapy Approach: Experts of Diverse Orientations Explore the Paradigm Prism*, edited by Francine Shapiro, 57–83. Washington, DC: American Psychological Association Press, 2002.

————. "Posttraumatic Therapy in the Age of Neuroscience." *Psychoanalytic Dialogues* 12, no. 3 (2002): 381–92.

Volf, Miroslav. *The End of Memory: Remembering Rightly in a Violent World*. Grand Rapids, MI: Eerdmans Publishing Company, 2006.

von Balthasar, Hans Urs. "The All-embracing Motherhood of the Church." In *The Office of Peter and the Structure of the Church*, translated by Andrée Emery, 183–225. San Francisco: Ignatius Press, 1986.

————. "Woman's Answer." In *Theo-Drama: Theological Dramatic Theory*. Vol. 3, *The Dramatis Personae: The Person in Christ*, translated by Graham Harrison, 283–360. San Francisco: Ignatius Press, 1992.

Wasserstein, Bernard. *Israelis and Palestinians: Why Do They Fight? Can They Stop?* New Haven, CT: Yale University Press, 2003.

Williams, H. A. *Tensions: Necessary Conflicts in Life and Love*. Springfield, IL: Templegate, 1977.

Wolmark, Jenny, ed. *Cybersexualities: A Reader on Feminist Theory, Cyborgs, and Cyberspace*. Edinburgh: Edinburgh University Press, 1999.

Woodward, Kenneth L. *Making Saints: How the Catholic Church Determines Who Becomes a Saint, Who Doesn't, and Why*. New York: Simon and Schuster, 1990.

Young, Robert J. C. *Colonial Desire: Hybridity in Theory, Culture and Race*. London: Routledge, 1995.

Index